Making Multimedia in the Classroom

Multimedia authoring offers a motivating and imaginative approach to subject matter where students can develop skills in group work and problem solving. This teachers' guide explores the process of students authoring multimedia presentations on computer using images, text, sound, animation and video, as an integrated part of their curriculum work. It offers a theoretical basis, detailed practical advice and many classroom examples.

Each chapter covers a different aspect of multimedia authoring including:

planning multimedia into the curriculum
considering audience, interactivity and design
classroom management of the project
assessment and evaluation
choosing software and resources.

This book encourages teachers to be imaginative about their subject and gives an important strategy for student motivation. It comes with a CD ROM which can be used in the classroom as an introduction to multimedia work.

Essential reading for all primary and secondary teachers and trainee teachers who wish to maximise the positive effects of multimedia in the classroom.

Vivi Lachs is an advisory teacher for ICT. In 1997 she was awarded a Winston Churchill Travelling Fellowship for multimedia in science.

To be

Making Multimedia in the Classroom

A teachers' guide

Vivi Lachs

London and New York

First published 2000
by RoutledgeFalmer
11 New Fetter Lane, London EC4P 4EE

Simultaneously published in the USA and Canada
by RoutledgeFalmer
29 West 35th Street, New York, NY 10001

RoutledgeFalmer is an imprint of the Taylor & Francis Group

© 2000 Vivi Lachs

Typeset in Sabon by
Keystroke, Jacaranda Lodge, Wolverhampton
Printed and bound in Great Britain by
TJ International Ltd, Padstow, Cornwall

British Library Cataloguing in Publication Data
A catalogue record for this book is available from the British Library

Library of Congress Cataloging in Publication Data
A catalogue record for this book has been requested

ISBN 0–415–21684–2

The work described in this book was possible due to the enthusiasm of students from the London borough of Hackney, and the commitment of their teachers.

This book is dedicated to creative students, resourceful teachers and challenging schools.

It is also dedicated to my father, Henry, who has been ever-supportive and an inspiration to me, and who sadly died while this book was in progress.

Contents

Screen shots

Colour section

The colour section is between pages 92 and 93

Figures and table

Figures

Table

Plates

Acknowledgements

Many people have been involved in my professional and academic work on multimedia authoring. They have all, directly or indirectly contributed to this book. The adults goaded and encouraged me to write, they read and re-read chapters and discussed and argued with me, planting ideas that I either developed or ignored. The students let me learn by watching them and were eager to tell me quite clearly what they thought of multimedia authoring. All this help was challenging, supportive, amusing and invaluable.

Thanks to:

Julian Sefton-Green (Weekend Arts College), Roger Frost (freelance trainer and writer) and Merlin John (*Times Educational Supplement*) for being pushy, encouraging and getting me writing;

Simon Spain (KidsOwn) and Tony Wheeler (TAG Developments) for idealistic and energising conversations;

Clare Johnson (QCA), Diana Freeman (Advisory Unit Computers-in-Education), Bronwen Evans (secondary English teacher), Tracy Atherton (primary school teacher), Geoff Strack (Independent ICT consultant) and Matt Wingate (TAG Developments) for meticulous reading and comments;

Deryn Watson, Dylan Wiliam and Margaret Cox of Kings' College, London for asking me questions and making me think harder;

Farquhar McKay (Hackney Education Business Partnership) for ongoing encouragement and Suresh Jethwa (independent ICT consultant) of Hackney Education for professional support;

Tom Baird (TAG Developments) for technical support with humour and Jody Press (The Final Touch) for website design;

Nina Stibbe, Jude Bowen, Sally Carter and Helen Fairlie, my helpful and chatty editors; and

The London Borough of Hackney, the Hackney Primary and Specialist Support Team, Hackney Education Business Partnership, and Hackney Urban Regeneration Projects for all these years.

Particular thanks to students and teachers in the following Hackney schools: Amherst, Baden Powell, De Beauvoir, Gainsborough, Harrington Hill, Holy Trinity, Kingsmead, Laburnum, Lauriston, Mandeville, Millfields, Queensbridge, Randal Cremer, Sebright, Simon Marks, St Dominic's Infants, St Dominic's Juniors, St John the Baptist,

St Monica's, and William Patten primary schools, and Cardinal Pole, Clapton, Hackney Free and Parochial, Haggerston and Kingsland secondary schools.

And to my parents, family and friends for intellectual and emotional support.

How to use this book

This book is a guide for subject teachers giving an overview of the elements needed to teach students of all ages how to produce multimedia in the classroom. Most chapters are set out in three sections. The first section, *Thinking about . . .* , gives some background ideas offering a theoretical perspective on the subject. This is followed by a number of examples of multimedia authoring in the classroom where students and teachers speak for themselves. The final section, *In practice . . .* , contains practical ideas and suggestions for a successful project. With this format the book can be read from beginning to end for an overview, or it can be dipped into to find the particular aspects that are immediately relevant, picking and choosing the ideas that work well and developing on them as more experience is gained. For example Chapter 6 looks at design issues and Chapter 9 looks at collecting information. These do not need to be read in this order as they may not necessarily be used with a class of students in this order. Chapters 13 and 14 give more detailed classroom examples focusing on young students and students with special needs. Chapter 15 gives teachers a voice to describe their development through using multimedia authoring a number of times with different classes. The final chapter advises on what to look for in effective classroom software, but is essentially about pedagogy and does not recommend any particular programs.

The CD ROM that comes with the book includes presentations described in the examples sections. Some of these will be short excerpts from a longer piece and some will be complete multimedia projects.

Book updates, how to contact the author, other useful websites and information on how to buy Hackney students' CD ROMs can be found on the author's website at: **www.hackney-making-multimedia.org.uk**

About the author

Vivi Lachs is an advisory teacher for ICT (Information and Communication Technology) in the London Borough of Hackney. Her background is in teaching Drama and English in secondary school and working with primary and secondary students with Special Educational Needs. As an advisory teacher for ICT she has had six years' experience of multimedia authoring in schools, working in classrooms in partnership with teachers on their first multimedia authoring projects. This creative engagement with both the technology and subject matter aimed to raise achievement in both these areas and to encourage teachers to continue using multimedia authoring as a teaching style. As a Winston Churchill Fellow in 1997, she had the opportunity to observe and learn from multimedia authoring in science in American and Canadian schools, and wrote articles about multimedia in the UK and abroad for the *Times Educational Supplement*. The examples described in the book and shown on the CD ROM are all projects she has been involved with, and the quotes from teachers and students were from her interviews and discussions with them.

Chapter 1

Introduction

Imagine walking around a Tudor maze with tall green hedges and narrow paths when your gaze is pulled to an object lying on the ground. As you bend down to pick up a golden crown you are transported to a meeting with King Henry VII who tells you about himself and his successful battles before sending you back to the maze. You continue walking, passing objects such as drums and stocks and pictures of people pinned on the hedges and every time you get curious and touch one of them, you are played Elizabethan music and shown the instruments, or find yourself in the crowd watching a gory beheading, or are introduced to Catherine of Aragon or Sir Walter Raleigh and told their stories before being returned, again trying to find your way around the maze. And then, as is so typical of mazes, you come to a dead end. There is a loud boom which startles you and you do not know where to go, but on a signpost there is a map of the whole maze, which lets you work out where you are.

No, this is not a costume role play and paperchase at Hampton Court, and no it is not fantasy or magic. This is multimedia made by students for students. Ten- and eleven-year-old student authors designed and made an interactive game describing what they had learned about the Tudors from more traditional classwork, and in the process learned a lot more than history (see Screen shot 1.1).

And now imagine walking around a classroom watching a group of students sitting round a table discussing a plan of a maze that is half formed in front of them. They have drawn boxes showing different screens of the maze, linked with arrows. They are trying to decide where to put images of the crown and the stocks to link with other screens of information, and if they should have any pictures of objects in the dead-end sections. As you look around your gaze is drawn to the two computers at the other side of the room. You see one student linking up a screen of the maze to a screen on vintners and another student scanning in a picture of children playing Tudor games. You walk across the classroom passing a student taking a picture with a digital camera of another student dressed in Tudor clothes. You pass a table where a student is reading a book on Tudor lifestyle, another is drawing some Tudor instruments and a third is writing text about Anne Boleyn on to a portable word processor. There is a loud drum beat, which startles you and as you turn you see two students at a computer recording the sound of a march.

This is a multimedia authoring classroom where students are involved in a creative and imaginative approach to learning history. It is a vibrant environment encouraging group work, flexible thinking and problem solving. Students are working on a whole class project that they are already proud of. Teachers are always looking for new

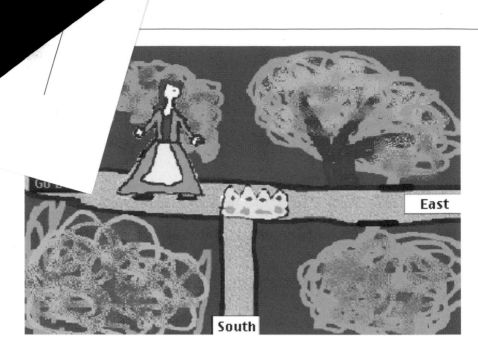

East

South

Screen shot 1.1 A screen from *The Tudor maze*, showing the user as a Tudor girl walking along singing to herself and coming across a crown. Clicking on the crown will link to a screen of information on Henry VIII. This complete presentation is on the CD ROM.

approaches to teaching subject information that will motivate students to research, study, write, make links between areas of knowledge and stimulate them to use their initiative and find out things for themselves. Multimedia authoring can be seen as a strategy for learning that can encourage these aims, and in this way can be used in any subject in the curriculum where there are ideas to be presented – whether factual or fictional, scientific or inventive.

What is multimedia?

Multimedia is essentially a presentation and communication tool. Multimedia programs, whether an encyclopaedia on CD ROM or a school website on the Internet are made up of three aspects; multimedia, hypertext and interactivity. This important jargon, although confusing if unfamiliar, is essential to describing the process of students using computers in the classroom. In order to understand the nature of multimedia and to consider the practical ideas needed to make multimedia, students and teachers will find it easier to use language that describes the medium clearly. This jargon is easily picked up by students and increases their ability to communicate what they are doing.

1. Multimedia

Multimedia is the mixture of different media. We see it around us all the time. Writing an illustrated story uses text *and* images, cartoons use animation *and* sound, talking

Crime	Punishment
Heresy (wrong religious ideas)	Burnt at the stake
Theft of apples	Rotten veg thrown at them
Fighting in the street	Serious whipping
Being very drunk and singing	Locked in stocks for a day
murdering, robbing and treason	beheading or hanging by the neck.

Go back to maze

Chop the head off

Screen shot 1.2 Going around the maze, clicking on a picture of stocks will link to this screen on crime and punishment. The screen is a combination of media; textual information accompanied by an animated beheading and a student shouting 'off with your head!'.

with your hands uses language *and* movement. Multimedia in a computer context has come to mean mixing more than two media. This can be seen in other creative settings. A theatre production uses language *and* movement *and* props *and* scenery *and* lighting. Television uses sound *and* film which in itself is action *and* sound. Multimedia on computers is the combination of text, images, sound, animation and video. The word combination is important because multimedia can create an integrated form where no one individual medium has supremacy. The text need not simply be accompanied by pictures and sound, as each medium can add to the whole understanding and effect of the multimedia experience (see Screen shot 1.2). The importance of this combination is that difficult and abstract concepts can be communicated concurrently in a number of ways, for example a three-dimensional animation can be explored while a voice-over explanation can point out particular details, each medium reinforcing and assisting in the understanding. This combination of media will be considered in Chapters 6 and 9.

2. Hypertext/hypermedia

Hypertext is a word coined in the 1960s which refers to the way that text on the screen can be linked to other text accessed by a mouse click. This is clearly seen on the Internet where hypertext links are shown by a different text colour, and clicking on the relevant words will transfer the user to a screen of connected information. The word hypertext only refers to linking text and is a precursor to the more inclusive term hypermedia.

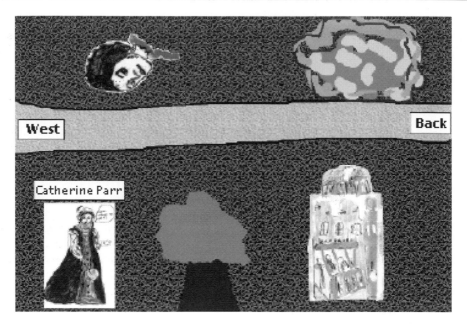

Screen shot 1.3 A screen of the maze. Clicking on the characters or the monastery will link to information screens about them.

Hypermedia refers to the way multimedia screens of information (such as paths of our Tudor maze) are linked together. The links can be accessed by clicking on images, icons, videos, etc., and this link will be to another screen of multimedia information. In the Tudor maze the hypermedia links are images of a crown, a drum and pictures of characters, and clicking on these images makes the screen dissolve into a connecting screen of relevant information. The crown links to information about Henry VII; stocks link to information about punishment – the symbolic representation of royalty or the law making connections in the student's mind.

The important consideration in the 'hyper' aspect of hypertext or hypermedia is that the connections are not necessarily linear. In one screen of the Tudor maze there may be two possible directions to go in and three pictures to click on: clicking on a 'button' that says 'west' will take you to a screen showing the next part of the path in the maze and clicking on a button that says 'back' will take you to the previous screen; clicking on the various pictures will link to screens of information about those characters or objects. This makes it possible to read or play the piece in a number of different ways. This non-linear nature of multimedia (sometimes called 'associative'), offers a way of presenting information by looking for how different aspects link together. It can produce parallel lines of thought set up in a non-hierarchical way. This makes hypermedia very different to more traditional linear writing found in books. Non-linear texts do not move left to right, down the page and turn over and do not necessarily have a beginning, middle and end. From one screen there can be any number of options in terms of information to find or storyline to follow. This creates an unusual narrative that is different to what teachers and students are used to in written text, but may be familiar to students from interactive computer games. The associative structure of multimedia authoring is built up by using 'buttons' or 'hot spots' on the screen that define an area to be clicked on. The monastery and images of characters in Screen shot 1.3 have invisible buttons behind the image. 'Back', and 'West' are visible buttons which link to connecting maze paths. This structure will be considered in more detail in Chapter 7.

The word *hyper*media describes both the mixing of different media and the non-linear structure. In education the term *multi*media tends to be substituted even though multimedia does not necessarily imply non-linearity. To be consistent with education usage I will use the term multimedia, but I am actually referring to non-linear environments.

3. Interactivity

A computer game is designed for a person to play in an interactive way, that is the user will have a degree of control of the narrative and direction of a story by clicking with the mouse on buttons and moving around the screen. The student will interact with the information and possibly with other students and this may include answering questions in a quiz, dragging objects across the screen and finding passwords as well as considering ideas and trying to solve problems (see Screen shot 1.4). Interactivity will be considered in Chapter 8.

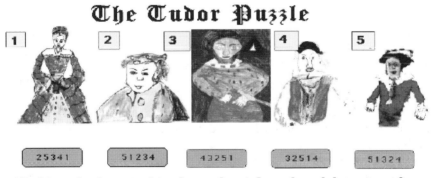

The Tudor Puzzle

Click on the button that shows the right order of the reign of the Tudor monarchs to get your reward. If you choose the wrong one you will be punished!

Screen shot 1.4 A Tudor interactive quiz where the player needs to choose the correct answer to reach the end of the maze. If the incorrect answer is chosen the player is sent back to the stocks in the middle of the maze.

Why multimedia authoring?

Multimedia is most commonly used in the classroom where students read and play professionally made CD ROM stories, or search for information in an electronic encyclopaedia and on the Internet. This is mainly passive, where the students are reading, listening, watching and taking in information on the screen. Even though there may be a degree of interactivity and control in student choice of direction, where to go in the story or what information to access, the autonomy and decision making comes within a very specific framework. The material is already there and the student's job is to access that knowledge, find answers to questions posed, maybe even redefining how the information links together – but not making it. These programs can be a useful way of reinforcing information in a different, new and exciting form which gives a greater degree of flexibility to the learner and can also be a strong motivator. However only *using* multimedia is not essentially creative.

Constructivist psychologists writing about cognition and education argue that people learn by making meaning. The learning process is only effective when meaning is constructed by learners themselves. If the students are doing the creating, they own the information they process more than if they simply find it. Papert (1991), from the Massachusetts Institute of Technology (MIT), wrote about *constructionism*. This is a development of the idea of constructivism in that he sees the importance of children making their own artefact of something that has a real reaction in the world. A multimedia program does this because students will be making the piece for someone to use. Some American researchers in hypermedia authoring are convinced of the importance of the constructive possibilities of the medium. Palumbo and Bermudez (1994) argue for the need for student involvement in multimedia creation to be active so that they become the 'builders of knowledge, inherently challenged to create new insights from the information provided' (p. 185). This implies that without the reader's absorbed and active attention and participation, the medium is not a challenging one. Lehrer *et al.* (1994) suggest that creating hypermedia documents for themselves gives learners 'the opportunity to see knowledge in a fundamentally new way, as a result of their constructive efforts rather than as a set of givens from their teacher and text' (p. 248). They also argue that the learners become much more involved and interested in the project, developing 'critical standards for knowledge'. This involvement with the nature of information, the structure of information, the connections between ideas, the design of an integrated way of communication and the consideration of how that communication can be received and used are all higher order thinking skills that students can develop through multimedia authoring.

This book will consider how students can actively engage with *making* multimedia, not simply *using* multimedia made by others, but by *creating* it themselves. Students *authoring* multimedia become software designers and this opens a number of avenues for learning additional skills and concepts at the same time as learning the subject matter they are presenting. This book is therefore designed for both primary teachers and secondary subject teachers wanting to integrate multimedia authoring into subjects in the curriculum from early years and throughout secondary education. It will consider what learning is happening through descriptions of classroom practice and interviews with teachers and students which will be put into context by some theoretical perspectives on these ideas. The practical aspects of the book will explain the process from initial planning to evaluation, giving advice and ideas on how to fit multimedia authoring into the curriculum, what ideas need to be discussed and considered by the class and how this can be organised in the classroom. The examples will show both successes and difficulties that can suggest models to copy and pitfalls to avoid.

The authoring process

Multimedia authoring is a creative process allowing students to find novel and interesting ways to express their ideas. They will need to view information critically and make decisions about what is important. They will come up against problems such as wanting to make the program do something that is beyond their abilities, which they will need to solve by using imagination and compromise. During this process students will need to consider the three elements described above; how to design multimedia as an integrated whole, how to create the non-linear environment and how to make the piece interactive and usable by an audience. In making a program rather than using one, the consideration of audience and communication will be paramount and will be discussed further in Chapter 5. The process of authoring will bring into play a number of other important considerations listed below and discussed in detail with examples in relevant chapters.

The students will need to consider:

- what to communicate
- who the audience is
- how to plan the piece out
- what the audience have to do and how to create these interactive elements
- which medium to use for which piece of information
- how screens will link together
- what they need to research
- how to work together with others
- how to criticise their work
- how to respond to criticism.

Although in terms of constructivist theory, it is the students who are the knowledge builders and in this case the software designers, the teachers need to be actively involved at every stage. There may need to be an amount of direct teaching of software and ideas around authoring, however the main role will be of analytical critic who will encourage students to reflect on what they are doing, try out new things and be imaginative during the process of collecting data, composing an argument, writing a story, and creating artwork.

Teachers will also need to consider:

- why they are using multimedia authoring
- where they want to put it into the curriculum
- where the computers will be located
- how long they will give to the project
- how they will work with the whole class, groups, pairs or individuals
- whether they will have multiple activities happening at the same time (as in the Tudor maze) or whether the class will be working on the same activities
- how they will introduce the students to the relevant ideas and concepts
- how it will work in practice
- how they will assess the process
- how they will evaluate the product.

These elements for consideration may not all be appropriate or relevant every time students author multimedia in the classroom. The first time students have worked in this way, there will need to be discussions and direct teaching on skills and ideas that may not need to be repeated a second time, but refined and developed.

Multimedia authoring or web authoring?

An interactive multimedia presentation can be delivered to an audience on a CD ROM or it can be made into a website and put on the Internet. CD ROM technology and web technology currently offer different types of presentation, however these two aspects are merging. As web authoring technologies advance, access to complex and sophisticated functions will become easier for non-technical and student users in a similar way that some multimedia authoring programs are already easy for students to use.

Students authoring multimedia for their own computer or to put on to a CD ROM is essentially about the imaginative presentation of curriculum work as an interactive program or game. As CD ROMs can store large quantities of information to be accessed quickly, these interactive games can use large full screen images, animations and video. They can use text and sound embedded in the visual experience of the piece as an integrated component, and special effects – such as rolling credits, pop-up text and graphics, text writing automatically and a variety of screen transitions. Some particular special effects make the piece interactive, such as the ability to make graphics or text 'dragable'. This enables the user to move an image around the screen or rotate a three-dimensional object, and so create a game, quiz or exploration. In multimedia authoring software designed for young people, these special effects are simple to construct. They can therefore enhance the options and creativity of how the subject matter is conceptualised and assist in communicating what they are trying to say, rather than being a project on how to create multimedia special effects.

Web authoring can also do this but it is currently more difficult for two reasons. First, the speed of information transfer on the Internet is restricted by the bandwidth of the cables and wires that are linking computers across the world. As large images and animations can take time to download, putting a multimedia piece on the web can cause long delays on moving from screen to screen. Generally, the larger the image, the longer it takes to come up on the computer screen, so full screen images with superimposed text and sound are not a good idea although small images and animations work well. Second, the software for web authoring would need a knowledge of JAVA programing to produce the more complex interactive features mentioned above in multimedia authoring.

The real power of web authoring lies in a different arena. The World Wide Web is a massive and growing database of structured and unstructured information where companies, schools and individuals put up screens of information for others to see. An individual's or school's website will be linked together with an internal structure so that a user can view the information with ease; however any web page can be linked to any other web page outside the specific website. This makes the World Wide Web as a whole a mass of information linked together allowing an infinite number of routes through the information. Web authoring can be seen therefore, not as creative programs, games and projects but more specifically about communicating and sharing ideas and information. A school website may have educational information, details on the school and display students' work, but also may include a forum for parents to e-mail teachers, for students to e-mail each other, for homework lines and bulletin boards of information. It can also provide the framework for a structured learning environment, where students and teachers can share ideas and examples of best practice, thus creating a virtual school community where communication and education can happen outside school hours.

Although web authoring is currently restricted in the use of multimedia by the bandwidth of Internet connections, these two technologies are combining and new software is emerging so that multimedia authoring can happen more easily on the web. This software will have all the advantages of full screen interactive multimedia as well as the possibilities for communication and collaboration offered by the web. For now the compromise is putting small multimedia projects on to a website running within a graphics box. This means that on a website where a school might display a student's drawing, it could display a graphic box containing a multimedia presentation. The user could then choose to download any software or 'plug-in' needed to run the multimedia piece and view it (albeit slowly) from their own computer.

At the time of writing, it will be necessary to decide in advance whether you will use multimedia authoring to make curriculum software (CD ROM) or web authoring to make a website, however the principles and classroom practice contained in this book will be pertinent to either way of working.

Hackney

The Tudor maze, described above, was one of over 40 multimedia projects run in classrooms in primary and secondary schools in the inner-London borough of Hackney. Hackney is a large borough with a range of people of different cultures, religions and ethnicity living side by side with more than 50 languages spoken. Students bring this variety of experience into their schoolwork, which is rich and vibrant. Hackney is also one of the most economically deprived areas of the country where the majority of students are from working-class families who are among the lowest earners in the UK. It has many inner-city problems such as drugs, poor housing and high unemployment. Regeneration projects are tackling these issues in the community and in schools. The school students in Hackney are lively and creative and have shown a great willingness to be involved in multimedia authoring projects. Their imagination shines through and in this area they have produced work that has exceeded the best in the country. Teachers in Hackney need to be committed and have a wide repertoire of teaching strategies. The teachers' willingness to participate in trying out new ideas is what has contributed to the success of Hackney students in multimedia authoring across the curriculum. The student authored multimedia projects span English, literacy, science, history, geography and technology, and are the work of students ages 4–17 working both in small groups and as whole classes within curriculum time. Over five years this work has been produced onto seven CD ROMs which have been used by other students, teachers and in homes in Hackney, nationally and internationally. Viewing and playing curriculum games produced by other students is an extremely useful motivator for students to produce their own and they are used for this purpose in Hackney schools. Although the work culminated in CD ROMs, some pieces could have become websites, but the large majority are too complex for students to author as websites. In the future, as Hackney schools come on-line, some multimedia work is being authored specifically for websites.

Chapter 2

Planning a project into the curriculum

Where in the curriculum does multimedia authoring fit? As multimedia authoring is a style of teaching and learning it can fit anywhere in the curriculum where images and animation can enhance students' understanding of a subject, or where presenting many aspects together in a non-hierarchichal way is appropriate. There are many times in the curriculum where an added extension to the work would be a bonus. For example in a technology class on structures students built towers out of newspaper to find one strong enough to hold some Easter eggs. The classroom ended up littered with unsuccessful as well as successful attempts. It would be useful to find a way of recording these attempts so that different pairs could see each other's process, not just the final product. In a geography class on earthquakes students read from a textbook about different ways in which p and s waves move. They drew their own diagrams giving explanations in words. It would be better if they could animate them and show the actual movement and the teacher could really see if they had understood. In a history class on the Anglo-Saxons students listened to tales of King Arthur, they wrote their own with pictures and read them out to the class. It would be a faithful reproduction if they could produce a permanent display of that work including the students' voices reading the stories. In an English class on the *Merchant of Venice* students watched videos showing different ways of performing one scene. They discussed which one they preferred and why. It would be a useful extension of their individual work if they could put all their multiple interpretations together and get a sense that a play can be performed in many ways which will bring out different aspects of the meaning.

All these additions could be done with multimedia authoring. This chapter will consider English, science, history and geography and offer suggestions of where multimedia authoring could contribute to these subjects. Although listed by subject, the ideas are transferable and could fit anywhere in the curriculum, so that any subject specialists or primary teachers might find the ideas from another subject useful. The possibilities are endless as they are creative and individual and these suggestions are only the tip of an iceberg intended to spark off teachers' own ideas. There are four specific examples shown in the screen images and these are presented in full on the CD ROM. Although this book considers using multimedia authoring within subject teaching, there will be many ICT skills taught and learned in the process. There is a final section to this chapter which looks at how multimedia authoring can fit into the National Curriculum for England and Wales.

English and literacy

English work involves understanding and communicating by reading, writing, speaking and listening. It involves creative thinking where new ideas are produced, and old ideas are reformulated, such as retelling stories, discussing ideas and forming opinions. Work is produced in a variety of styles, and multimedia authoring adds an interesting new approach. The use of sounds and images extends a written text to a multimedia text. The use of branching stories or adventure games offering a number of choices extends the concept of linear narrative to a non-linear narrative. This non-linearity allows time to be frozen, slowed down or accelerated encouraging presentation of different types of work. Multimedia literacy is the ability to read a text of images, sound and written words, while deciding where to read first. Authoring multimedia in the English curriculum asks students to create this new literacy.

EXAMPLE 1: COMPOSING ALTERNATIVE NARRATIVES

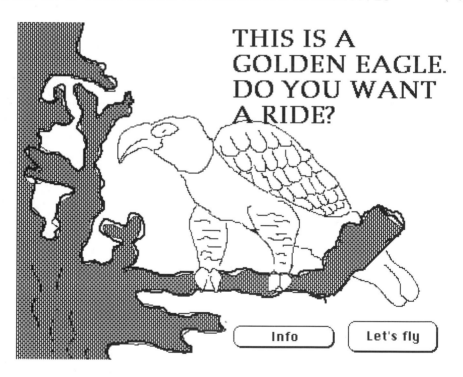

Screen shot 2.1. Find the tigers is an adventure game designed by four year-6 students (10 and 11 year olds). It is a story with multiple pathways where the user must decide where to go to find tigers and disarm hunters. This was part of a project on creating alternative narratives for an audience of younger students. (More details on how the students planned out this project are in Chapter 7, example 1). The full presentation is on the CD-ROM.

Ten ideas for multimedia into English and drama

1   Write a character's words from a play beneath a drawn image and add a spoken voice-over with the character's thoughts. (This could begin as a role play off the computer.)

2   Compose stories with alternative endings where the user will be able to choose the ending they want.

3   Write out a poem being studied in class, adding images or animations to give it an interpretation and a voice-over rendition.

4   Create an on-screen class magazine or moving newspaper which includes interactive quizzes, photographs and sound interviews. This could be done over a length of time at one computer where each student or pair of students adds to the work of previous students.

5   Each pair of students puts forward one side of an argument in three screens. When completed, show to students working on the other side of the argument, and debate how influential they find the multimedia portrayal.

6   Display a number of alternative interpretations of a scene in a play by hearing the speech dramatised as a role play from different motivations which are accessed one after the other by clicking different buttons.

7   Draw out parts of a theatre set and make them dragable so that students can try out different arrangements by moving the objects around. Ask students to save their arrangement and add text to explain why it is an appropriate set.

8   Make adventure stories designing a non-linear narrative giving choice of direction to the reader.

9   Make flashbacks in a story by making the screen dissolve into another screen. Consider having different screen transitions for moving forwards and backwards in time, letting the user jump through time.

10   Consider the characters in a novel and put images of them around the screen. Describe them in words or sound to be accessed by clicking on these pictures.

Science

Science work involves exploring and engaging with phenomena and processes of the natural world. Students do this by a mixture of questioning and experimenting in order to understand scientific concepts. This is a creative and dynamic process, however students often present their findings with text and diagrams and explain experiments in words. The objects they explain are three dimensional and can be complex, and the concern is often with processes which are ongoing and dynamic. Multimedia authoring can make abstract diagrams become more concrete and three-dimensional explanations and experiments become animated. In this way students can show that they understand the complete nature of what they are presenting, and doing it will help them clarify that understanding for themselves.

EXAMPLE 2: ANIMATING DYNAMIC SYSTEMS

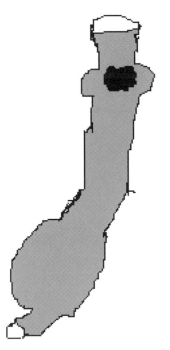

Screen shot 2.2 Science: digestion

swallow food

This is an animation of peristalsis in the gullet. It's an animation of when you swallow something. When you squeeze the top the foc gets pushed down towards the intestines. The oesophagus changes shape according to the size of the food.

Screen shot 2.2 Science: digestion. A year-8 class (12 and 13 year olds) made a multimedia presentation on digestion and blood circulation. They worked in pairs, each taking a different process to animate and describe in one or two screens. These were then pulled together to make a general explanation of these systems. The full presentation is on the CD ROM.

Ten ideas for multimedia into science

1 Animate things we can see such as a solar eclipse, plant growing, colour changing in an experiment, shadows changing as the sun moves.

2 Animate things we cannot see such as the electron movement in an electric circuit, movement of blood through the heart, cell division.

3 Take photographs from different angles of a model of DNA and animate it to revolve with a voice over explanation.

4 Draw a labelled diagram of the digestive system with the possibility of zooming in to get close-ups of particular parts.

5 Draw a series of pictures about forces, and make arrows for the user to drag to show what forces are acting on each occasion.

6 Use animations to slow down or speed up processes; for example, animating photographs taken each day of a seed growing to speed up the process, or drawing an eye in different positions to show a slowed down blink.

7 Draw out different parts of the life cycle of a flowering plant, make them dragable and put them out of order so that the user has to order them correctly.

8 Draw different materials which, when a user clicks on them, have text appearing to explain some of their properties.

9 Draw parts of the water cycle on different screens and show what happens when water heats and cools, by moving from screen to screen.

10 Show an atom by drawing images on separate screens and zooming in to smaller and smaller images with a mouse click.

History

History work involves understanding past events, finding out what occurred, what motivated people to do certain actions, putting it into a relevant context and considering evidence and debating how it affects the present. Although time is linear, considering the past and how it affects the future is not necessarily a linear activity. Using multimedia authoring separate pieces of evidence could be presented in a non-hierarchical way where time could go backwards and forwards and the choice of where to go in the timeline is up to the user.

EXAMPLE 3: USING A HISTORICAL STORY TO UNDERSTAND HISTORICAL CONCEPTS

Screen shot 2.3 History: Persephone

A year-3 class (7 and 8 year olds) retold the story of *Persephone*. They drew out 12 screens telling the story with full screen images and text, then added an option to hear the story from different characters points of view. These perspectives were accessed by clicking on photographs of themselves dressed as the characters. Other members of the class looked at how old different things are in order to locate the Greeks in time. They also considered what things are true and what are not true, both about themselves and about the Greeks, in order to understand myths and different versions of the same story (and history). The full presentation is on the CD ROM.

Ten ideas for multimedia into history

1 Interactive timeline. Click on the date to see the events. Different students could take on a different date or event.

2 Historical characters. Click on a drawing of the character or a photograph of a student in role to hear them tell you about themselves.

3 Show events happening in different places at the same time by clicking on an interactive map.

4 Draw a series of maps changing over time as borders of countries changed.

5 Make a game where historical characters are drawn and made dragable for the user to put in the right order.

6 Make a hieroglyphic password to get into a pyramid to see what is inside.

7 Tell a fictional historical story using information about what life was like at the time. Put an anachronistic item on each screen which the user has to click on to link to information about how transport, clothing, etc. has changed.

8 Dress up in appropriate costume, photograph the characters and use them in a multimedia story with the students' voices speaking as the characters. Additional buttons could be added which will give the thoughts or motivation of each character.

9 Draw or photograph a historic building and go inside it by clicking to reveal what's indoors, drawn on separate screens.

10 Record students discussing the causes of the First World War to be accessed by clicking on specific characters, a map or symbolic references.

Geography

Geography work involves exploring our environment, local to our cities and countryside and global as our planet. It covers both people and places and how societies have changed over time. This involves very long passages of time and enormous geological events as well as local environmental issues of playgrounds, schools and roads. Using multimedia authoring, maps can become interactive, hiding text and sound and animations relevant to the subject. Time can be controlled and shown in a meaningful way.

EXAMPLE 4: CLIMATE ACROSS THE WORLD AND WHAT IT AFFECTS

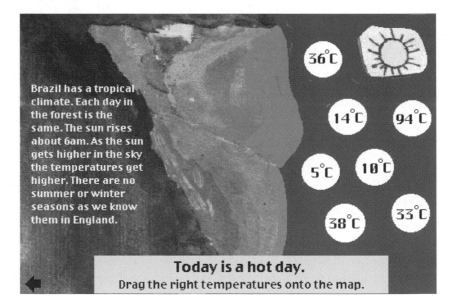

Screen shot 2.4 Geography: climate. A year-5 class (9 and 10 year olds) working on climate in different countries made a game as part of their piece where the user needed to drag the correct temperature on to the map. If they tried to drag the incorrect one they were given voice-over clues such as 'It's frrreeeezing', or 'Man, I's gonna fry'. The full presentation is on the CD ROM.

Ten ideas for multimedia into geography

1 Draw different types of maps of the same area on and off the computer, photographing or scanning to put them on the computer, where clicking on features gives more information.

2 Make animations of a slow processes such as continental drift or environmental change.

3 Draw or photograph a local high street where buildings and shops can be entered and explored, giving local and environmental information.

4 Make an interactive tourist brochure where you find out about features of different countries by clicking on the relevant pictures.

5 Show how weather changes over time by moving between screens.

6 Consider the best route for a new road by making items in the scene dragable and moving them around. Include local people and click on them to hear their views from interview or role play.

7 Draw rivers, channels and tributaries on different screens with information to be accessed from a main screen showing an aerial view.

8 Make an interactive exploration of the school, being able to enter classrooms and click on various items.

9 Set out different aspects of a real issue using photographs and scanned in newspaper clippings, with students adding their own or role played views in text or sound.

10 Consider local and global environmental issues animating relevant processes.

Setting objectives

The objectives you choose should be formalised and discussed with the students so that these criteria can be used when it comes to evaluating their work and assessing how well they went through the process. It is important to see it as part of ongoing curriculum development. With this in mind, any objectives will need to be considered by each individual teacher in line with literacy, numeracy, curriculum objectives and exam syllabi.

Early objectives for the students might include that they will:

- become familiar with the software
- design two multimedia screens
- link these two screens together
- research information for these screens
- ensure that they can be used by someone else.

Further project objectives might include that students will:

- have a clear purpose for their piece
- plan out their piece showing links between cards
- plan out an interactive structure
- plan out rough designs for the screens
- consider who the audience is for their piece and use appropriate language
- work collaboratively and co-operatively with other members of the class
- research appropriately from books, the Internet and real life information such as interviews
- be critical of the information they collect
- design, collect information and make screens of integrated media
- give critical feedback to fellow students
- evaluate the process and the final piece.

Multimedia authoring in the National Curriculum

Information and Communication Technology (ICT) is a compulsory subject in the National Curriculum of England and Wales, taught at all key stages. Although ICT is a subject on its own, the knowledge, understanding and skills taught as ICT are expected to be applied and developed across the curriculum (similar to numeracy and literacy). Indeed ICT is specified in the programmes of study of other subjects and is a part of a statement at the beginning of every single subject.

Different schools teach ICT in different ways. Secondary schools with specialist ICT teachers often teach discrete ICT elements in separate ICT classes, which then form the basis for its use across the curriculum. For example, a secondary school in Hackney teaches multimedia authoring in their timetabled ICT classes. The students choose the content for the piece (usually television or football), and they get to understand how the software works. They should then get the opportunity to use multimedia authoring as the ICT component of their science or languages classes. This could become more integrated by the ICT teacher and the subject teacher working together, so that rather than television or football, the content is English or PE. This integrated approach would mean ICT is used in the context of English or PE, however there would still be direct ICT teaching. In primary schools, with one teacher teaching all subjects, integrating ICT into the context of a subject is easier. For example, a primary school might use multimedia authoring in a history project, and in the course of learning the history, the students have specific lessons on how to use different aspects of the program, how to consider audience and interactivity, how to integrate different media, and other concepts behind multimedia authoring.

The National Curriculum document for ICT is set out in a number of themes which identify areas of learning and which chart the progression in these areas. Multimedia authoring is suggested explicitly as a possibility at key stage 2 (7–11 year olds), and specifically offered as a unit of the Qualifications and Curriculum Authority's Schemes of Work for Information Technology for year 6 (10–11 year olds). As this book will show, multimedia authoring can be effective throughout schooling for 4–18 year olds because creating curriculum presentations is something that can be developed and made more sophisticated as students become more skilled and effective at abstract thinking and presentation. The National Curriculum rarely states specific software tools, and it is very clear that multimedia authoring can contribute to ICT development across all key stages. In this section there are short descriptions of the four main National Curriculum themes with ideas of where multimedia authoring could fit into these themes and indeed develop them further.

1. Finding things out   This theme asks students to consider the nature of information and the purpose for which it is to be used, in an increasingly analytic and collaborative way, moving from simple gathering of information to a more complex understanding of the nature of its collection and use. Although this theme deals mainly with searching computerised data and information, it includes the need to search and collect information from non-electronic sources as well. In any multimedia presentation with a factual basis, information collection will need to be an integral part of the project. Students will need to make decisions about what they require, where to look for it, why they are using it and what their attitude is towards it. When an audience is involved, collecting information has a clear focus and they will need to set up their search bearing this in mind.

2. Developing ideas and making things happen   Part of this theme is the requirement for students to manipulate media in an increasingly complex way from simply using different media through collating their own multimedia to collaboratively deriving additional information. Multimedia authoring will require students to plan, edit and organise a presentation. Students can become critical analysts of other multimedia to help them develop presentations that increase in quality and progress from simply combining the media in an illustrative way, to completely integrating media they have created into an interactive multimedia presentation.

3. Exchanging and sharing information   This theme asks students to present their ideas, from a simple display of their work to a more complex consideration of how their work will be viewed and used by different audiences, and how taking this into account will affect the quality and purpose of what they do. This is particularly appropriate for multimedia authoring which involves the development of multimedia presentations or websites that are designed for particular audiences.

4. Reviewing, modifying and evaluating work as it progresses   This theme asks students to assess their ICT work critically. This progresses from a simple description of what they have done and what they will do, through to a reflection on how they have worked and a comparison to other ways of working, to an analysis and evaluation of effective use of ICT. This process of reviewing should be both collaborative and encourage individuals to develop initiative and independence. In multimedia authoring, students start by describing and explaining the process they have been through and the product they have created, and develop to analyse their own multimedia work and that of others in a critical way, suggesting improvements in an ongoing attempt to produce quality multimedia work. Towards the end of a project, students will consider audience feedback on their own work to ascertain whether they achieved their purpose. Students author multimedia most effectively when working in groups, collaborating and helping each other.

The National Curriculum orders end with level descriptions running from one to eight and an additional one for exceptional performance. In a few generalised sentences the level descriptions chart the progression as students develop the knowledge, understanding and skills specified in the orders.

Multimedia authoring across the curriculum

As explained above, using ICT is an important component in every subject. In secondary schools as a subject teacher you should be able to assume that the students are learning to use the programs in their ICT classes, and that your class does not need to concentrate on that aspect. Subject teachers will have alternative motives. In some subjects you may find that National Curriculum requirements for the subject could be fulfilled by using multimedia authoring, such as writing for different audiences in English. On the other hand, it may not be part of the science curriculum to make animated electric circuits, however, by animating scientific concepts, the teacher can get a sense of the students' understanding of those concepts. Teachers will need to decide where ICT helps learning in their particular subject. It may be that multimedia authoring is useful because it can be motivating for students, especially those who find learning and communicating difficult using more traditional methods.

Table 2.1 on pp. 24–5 charts a progression route for using multimedia authoring. This will fulfil parts of the National Curriculum requirements for ICT and the use of ICT in other subjects. It is not, however, linked to level descriptions as it starts pre-level one, and is intended to help teachers see how a multimedia authoring project can grow in quality of information and sophistication of design. It is a cumulative chart, so, for example, after the third stage of progression all pieces should have a clear purpose in mind, and by the sixth stage students should be planning interactive structures in detail on paper. This chart may be useful as part of a scheme of work.

Tips for starting

- First timers choose an area that you know well and do not be over-ambitious.
- Start small with a contained project over two or three lessons.
- Students can begin by considering how images, text and sound interact on one single screen.
- To start, have limited objectives until you get used to the medium.
- Give yourself as a teacher some objectives, such as learning the software or how to use the scanner.

Checklist

- Decide where multimedia authoring will fit into your curriculum time.
- Consider where it will fit into your subject, in England and Wales, taking the National Curriculum into consideration.
- Make specific objectives for the project for both students and teacher.

Table 2.1 Progression chart for multimedia authoring

Using multimedia and collecting information	Planning a piece and integrating different media	Consideration of audience and interactivity	Evaluation and discussion of work in progress
Use a multimedia CD ROM story that includes pictures and sound.	Move clipart and words around the screen in a ready made template.	Audience is themselves and the teacher.	Describe what happened in the story and where they had to click.
Change the order of a ready-made multimedia story by moving around images and text.	Using a story template, draw a picture and add words describing it.	Audience is themselves and the teacher.	Tell their story and describe what they did to make it.
Gather together images (their own computer-drawn and clipart) to use in a presentation.	Write a linear story using text, pictures and sound like an illustrated book.	Make the piece to be used in their own classroom for a specific purpose.	Describe what they have done and discuss other multimedia stories they have used on the computer.
Import images from other programs. Create artwork using different art media off the computer to be scanned in.	Write a multimedia story that has more than one possible ending.	Make the story for another class in the school thinking about making it entertaining and interesting.	Describe how the story was different to a book. Explain how images and sound contributed to their piece.
Collect information from electronic sources such as a digital camera and text processors.	Combine information in a non-linear format. Plan a storyboard of individual screens.	Make the piece for a younger class simple enough to understand and navigate.	Look at other multi-media work and discuss structure, interactivity and navigation.
Only collect information that is relevant to their purpose. Scan their own images on to the computer thinking about creating quality artwork.	Collaboratively plan a non-linear structure showing how screens link and detailing any interactive elements on individual screens.	Having a specific audience in mind, develop interactive features so that the audience has something to 'do' to play the game.	Consider the differ-ences between multimedia authoring and presenting this work in other ways. Discuss why *making* multimedia is different to *using* it.
Gather information from CD ROMs, the Internet, photographs and original work. Collect images for animation that need to be sequenced.	Use animation as an integrated part of the multimedia to explain an idea. Sequence the animation on paper.	Choose a known but unfamiliar audience, discuss how they can be considered, researching if necessary.	From trialling the piece with a sample audience, discuss what they noticed and how they might need to change their piece to make it work better.
Be critical about the quality of information they collect, and make decisions about what to use and in what way to present it.	Make clear plans that show navigation routes, interactive features and animation. Ensure that the media are more integrated than illustrative.	Develop interactivity by thinking about audience response to the ideas and content, and the balance of control: author/audience.	Discuss the importance of integrating the media rather than making illustrated books. Consider how different media are good for different purposes.

Table 2.1 continued

Using multimedia and collecting information	Planning a piece and integrating different media	Consideration of audience and interactivity	Evaluation and discussion of work in progress
Collect information from a larger variety of sources including interviews and e-mail transactions with relevant people. Ask questions carefully so correct information is gathered.	Use a variety of styles in combining the media. Consider the use of symbolic representation of ideas and ensure the piece is completely integrated.	Consider two different audiences such as students and parents at a parents' evening. Think about making the piece accessible to both audiences.	Discuss issues raised by the use of multi-media authoring. Consider their slant on the information as only one of many, and discuss the ethics of trying to convince people of your point of view.

Chapter 3

Group work and collaboration

Thinking about . . .

Group work is a familiar part of school activity where students work together to help each other, share and develop ideas, and learn the importance of being able to trust others and take responsibility. Vygotsky (a Russian psychologist working in the 1920s and 1930s) viewed learning as a social construction. He argued that learning takes place in the gap between what students can do on their own and what they can do with the help of an adult or more capable peer. He called this gap the 'Zone of Proximal Development' and saw it as a fertile ground for learning. An adult or more capable peer can help the learner learn by acting as a 'scaffold' (Wood, Bruner and Ross 1976). Just like a scaffold helps for a while during building construction and is then taken away and the building can stand on its own, so students and teachers can help other students in this process until those students no longer need their help. The implication of this theory is that learning is not a process that you do on your own, but something that happens within a social context, using language to communicate, and is therefore culture specific. One of the ways that this theory is implemented in the classroom is through group work.

Co-operative groups

One view of group work focuses on co-operation. In a co-operative group students work together in a highly structured way in order to develop co-operation skills. Each member of the group takes on a different role, such as scribe, designer, listener and so on. These roles are well defined and do not overlap. The idea is that the group will produce a joint outcome, with each group member having an individual part to play. This can be seen in a professional setting where designing a piece of software takes place within a design team. This team may include planners, developers, researchers, writers and animators. There are those who concentrate solely on creating interactive elements or on producing specific pieces of artwork, and those who work on creating the links needed for the piece to work as an integrated interactive presentation. There are people to correct text, check the accuracy of the information and check that the links run. It is a complicated process that involves many people with different skills, from artistic to organisational to computer and programing. Some team members will need an overview of the whole product, while others may only be brought in for specific stages. Sometimes team members will work together and sometimes alone. It may be that someone cannot perform their role until someone else has completed their section, so knowing what others have done is important and will give people a sense of where their input fits in with the whole piece. This communication may occur in team meetings, design diaries and detailed notes.

Two American educational researchers (Liu and Rutledge 1997) transferred this model to a multimedia authoring project with groups of 'at risk' 10th, 11th and 12th grade students (15–17 year olds). The students' task was to make history or science software for 5 year olds. They ran the project as if it were a multimedia production house, giving the students lots of input in explaining the design process. The students arranged roles for themselves, including a team manager who kept everyone on task and motivated, having group meetings and voting in order to make decisions. The researchers explained that 'although each member will have his/her distinctive role, the success of a hypermedia program depends on constant communication and understanding between team members and their working together to reach the goal' (p. 146).

Tightly defined co-operative groups use roles as a modus operandi, but co-operative activities happen all the time in the classroom where two students may be sitting together, lending each other equipment, chatting and helping with work. This less structured co-operative behaviour can be useful in hypermedia authoring, however students will still essentially be working individually. Working *together* takes collaboration.

Group collaboration

Collaboration describes the way a group communicates and works together. This can be part of a co-operative activity, but need not be a part of a co-operative group. A group working collaboratively may be working towards a similar outcome to that of a co-operative design team, however the process is different. Collaboration produces a joint product created from a shared understanding where the group is an arena for discussion and development. The collaboration between group members will allow people to hear other people's views, build on each other's ideas, make joint decisions and develop and learn in the process. Group members will not take on roles, they will all be involved in steering the course of the project and in doing a mixture of activities rather than confined to one. In collaboration each student will come up against other students' views. They will need to be able to argue their own point of view, explain their own understanding and work out how these different points of view can work together. This will involve compromise and flexibility as well as combining ideas. Collaborative working is particularly useful for something as creative as multimedia authoring where the interplay of ideas can greatly enhance the effectiveness of the multimedia presentation.

Collaboration can be mediated by a computer which supplies a good focus of attention. As more than one person can view the screen at the same time, the computer offers natural possibilities for students to work together, commenting on the information they are exploring or authoring, the images, sound and so on. When making a multimedia presentation students may be working together on creating the different media as generic designers who do everything from researching to designing screens to linking them together. Authoring multimedia requires a variety of skills such as drawing, concisely, clear speaking, having a good sense of design or clever ideas for a

Students will no doubt possess different skills and will want to do more of what they are good at, which gives an ideal opportunity for mixed ability groupings where everyone does not need to be expert at everything. Collaborative group work does not need to constrain students, who can work together on things they find difficult. This will give the opportunity for a class to experience group authorship and therefore group ownership, and a sense of cohesion as a group can have benefits that last beyond the individual project. As every class is made up of different people with different needs and abilities, these need to be taken into consideration. When organising groups it is important to address a number of issues.

Gender

There is a lot written about girls and computers. It is generally found that boys are more confident in using computers and, when working with girls, take control of the mouse and keyboard more of the time. In her research on gender and groups Underwood (1998) describes how girls-only groups collaborated and co-operated better than the boys-only or mixed groups. However when boys-only groups were told explicitly to co-operate they also made good performance gains. This should be taken into consideration when setting up groups so that girls are able to be hands-on and active and all students are helped to collaborate. This could be achieved by having single sex groups or by raising the issues with any groups. It is certainly important that group skills be taught.

English as an additional language (EAL)

Working on making a piece of software with a variety of media offers opportunities to communicate information in more than one way. Students may be able to describe ideas through image or animation even if they find it difficult to express it in English. The use of sound offers possibilities to add text in additional languages, written and spoken, which can raise the status of students' home languages. As part of a group, students with EAL can achieve more than they could on their own, and also feel part of the larger group experience.

Students with special educational needs (SEN)

Students with special educational needs often view themselves as failures and find it difficult to complete work. They tend to get praised less than other class members, and do not succeed as often. Being a part of a mixed group where the group outcome is what is seen can give these individuals the possibility of feeling *a part of* rather than *apart from* their classmates. Computers are seen to improve the concentration of students with SEN by giving them an external focus to their work and helping them produce work that is neat and readable. Two in-depth examples of multimedia authoring projects with groups of SEN students in mainstream schools will be described in Chapter 14.

Multimedia authoring can provide an opportunity for both co-operation and collaboration. The examples that follow show both the advantages and difficulties of group work in multimedia authoring projects.

Example 1: Balancing collaborative and co-operative activities

Project title: *Find the climate*
Project focus: How people and animals adapt to different climates
Curriculum area: Geography/Science
Age group: Year 5 (9–10 year olds)
Group structure: Whole class, small groups and pairs. Collaborative planning and computer work, individual artwork with students co-operating and helping each other with individual screens
Location: Classroom and small computer room
Time: One and a half hours a week for 9 weeks

Before this project began the teacher had designed the overall concept of the piece of work: a player who would travel to different areas of the world and find out information about climate, houses, clothing and animals. She had chosen the countries to represent different climate zones and described this structure to the whole class so that they had an overall feel of where their work would fit in. The project continued with whole class teaching and discussion both on the subject (climate and adaptation) and on the nature of multimedia (interactivity, computer games and audience). Only then was the class split into six groups, each working on one country. Their first task as a group was to plan out on paper how the aspects of their designated country would work as an interactive game and highlight what information they would need to research. The group plans had to have the same number of screens as group members so that each student could take responsibility for one screen. This planning task was a discussion activity where students had to listen to each other, decide which ideas they agreed on, and draw out a plan of linked screens to present to the class. All the groups went through a collaborative process of discussion and compromises, some more successfully than others. In some groups an articulate student would have most of the ideas and the others would agree, in others there were differences that needed negotiation. A boy in the Brazil group described how his group worked together:

> *We all had ideas. I had one about finding a monkey. One said this, one said that, we combined them together and made a game. But then SH had a different idea for a game and everyone else agreed with her, so we did that one.*

This group were able to build up an idea together, even if they did then drop it for another idea. In fact this group ended up using both ideas and having two separate game elements as part of their presentation.

The Kenya group had a difference of opinion as to what they wanted to do. One of the girls told me:

> *We couldn't agree. The boys only wanted to draw but the girls wanted to do something on fashion. So we decided that they could draw the clothes and then we'd make it into a game.*

Plate 3.1 A small group of students planning work off the computer while two other students are putting work on to the computer.

Although the girls' idea might have come out of their lack of agreement, it did end up as a fairly good compromise.

Each group had a designated table in their classroom to work on and a designated computer in the computer room. Students worked individually at their group tables researching from books or making artwork with paints or collage or crayons (see Plate 3.1). They generally helped each other, giving advice on colour or material. One student drew an outline of an igloo for another student who was having difficulty drawing, but was then able to paste cotton wool on to it himself. This co-operation may well have been fuelled by the students wanting their country to look good as a whole section. After each screen was completed the student or pair of students would scan their work into the computer and stick the original artwork on to their plan. They then worked in twos or threes at the computer, adding text and sound, linking screens together and making interactive features. Towards the end of the project, group members who had finished their screens worked on the general opening section that would link all the countries together.

The project had begun as a whole class direct teaching session, moved to small group collaboration in discussion and planning, then individual students worked co-operatively on artwork before pairs pulled the screens together at the computer again, collaborating on design of the screens and specific wording of the text. Finally at the end of the project the whole class came together to see all the countries linked together, comment on each others' work and consider if anything needed to be added to complete the piece. As students had been working in their groups for the project, this final whole class work brought the class to a recognition of the multimedia presentation belonging to everyone with each class member having made an important contribution. This was an upbeat session where students got excited as they were really impressed with the work done by their classmates which gave them a sense of pride and class ownership of the completed presentation.

Example 2: Difficulties with working in groups

Project title: *Genetic engineering and selective breeding*
Project focus: Preview to year 10 science work
Curriculum area: Science extension work
Age group: Year 9 (13–14 year olds)
Group structure: Pairs and groups of fours. Two students worked to a computer, so any group of four students split into two pairs for the computer work
Location: Computer room and science lab
Time: Two hours a week for 6 weeks. One hour in computer room, one hour in science lab

---

Before the students began this science project the teacher had divided the subject matter into different sections and made a list that he wrote up on the board. Each student chose a partner or a group of four (friendship, same sex groups) and one of the topics to work on. Each group or pair began the project by structuring their own section and finding out what they needed to research. They were given a small amount of time in class to draw out a plan of their multimedia presentation and asked to continue it together in their own time; however as this proved difficult logistically, most of the students did not produce good plans, if any, which meant that they needed to work it out it as they went along.

This particular year-9 group were bright and very lively. Their teacher described them as: *'Such a bunch of individuals that group work is not one of their strengths although collectively they're quite supportive in a naughty way'*. He had not done any group work with them before but had assumed that they had done group work in other subjects. As it happened the class found it difficult to work together and would have benefited from prior discussion on how to work in groups.

Despite their lack of experience, the students rose fairly well to the occasion. As pairs worked at the computers together, there was constant talk and discussion between them, on and off task. On-task talk was often collaborative discussion about the content of their presentation, for example which bits of information they were going to use or how to word a particular sentence. Other talk, although on task, was time wasting, focusing on minutiae of detail; for example, one pair discussing the design of a screen spent a long time deciding what colour gradients they should use as a background to their title page. This pair were so attracted by the features of the software that they had to be reminded of the science work. Making decisions was not always easy for pairs and sometimes many possibilities were tried before they chose one. The off-task talk tended to be general chatter while working, sometimes masquerading as co-operation where one student would go across the room ostensibly to help another student, but end up in conversation.

Four girls worked with fairly consistent concentration together in a group on genetically modified tomatoes. In an interview with three of them after the project, they spoke about how they worked together:

Student 1:   *Us three really contributed to the work, but M was just quiet and didn't do much.*
Student 2:   *We all put together ideas.*
Student 3:   *We all had points of view. We didn't want the same things, and M just said okay.*
Student 1:   *It was my idea that started it off, because I made a plan of how we would set out our cards.*
Student 2:   *And after, we used a magazine, explaining about genetically modified tomatoes.*
Student 3:   *We argued about colours, and argued about backgrounds, and argued about different buttons and drawings. Did we argue about the information?*
Student 2:   *It was the wording of the information we argued over.*
Student 3:   *And then we put it together into our masterpiece.*
Student 1:   *I didn't like the front page because the tomatoes were too small, so we redid it . . .*
Student 2:   *Everyone had their opinion.*
Student 1:   *It gave us more ideas.*
Student 3:   *It gave us more to think about.*
Student 1:   *Helped us improve our project.*
Student 3:   *If one had done this on their own, it wouldn't have come out as good as it is.*

The students felt very positive about their collaboration. The way they talked about arguing seems to suggest that there was a battle of wills over different people's opinions rather than a sharing of ideas, however they seemed to appreciate that the final outcome was a combined effort that was greater than the sum of its parts. Their science teacher saw a difference between the girls and the boys in this particular class:

> *The girls seemed to cope far better* [working in groups], *they naturally collaborate. The boys wanted to do funny things, animation and special effects. The girls were much more focused on task.*

One boys' group in the class was not assigned any one part of the subject matter, but was designated as the 'structure' group to make a title and menu screen which would link to each individual group. They spent most of their time thinking about how diverse pieces of information would link together. They needed an overview of all the other groups which meant talking to them. This group then drew a number of different plans before finding one that they felt would work. Two of the boys described what they had to do:

Student 1:   *One group was doing one section, but we could do bits from all different ones. We wanted to get it* [the structure] *down on paper and wrote it up on the board.*

Student 2:   *We did a spider diagram of all the things we wanted.*
Student 1:   *We put the ideas we thought would stand out the most and used them ones and took it further on to the computer.*
Student 2:   *We used a DNA strand on the front page, 'cos it's a genetics project and DNA is basically genetics, and there would be buttons going off to home pages of the sections and buttons going off into the different groups.*

Communication with the other groups was not so simple and this took some diplomacy. In fact, although the boys worked fairly efficiently amongst themselves, when it came to talking to other groups they were shy about asking them to co-operate and were not always successful:

Student 1:   *We had to go to other groups and say you must put a button here [to link up to the main menu], and they'd say it might look bad.*
Student 2:   *They had to work with us but the girls just said, go away.*

Most of the pair work in this project was collaborative. While working at the computer, students were designing the screens as they made them and researching as they wrote text. Although the lack of planning made the work more difficult and more time consuming, in some ways it added to the collaboration as students constantly needed to discuss the content and the links. However, because this class were not used to group work, they wasted a lot of time and worked slowly, resulting in some of the outcome being poor quality. Although the process may have taught the students an amount, the quality of the final product is important because it gives them a sense of pride. This class did not end with a sense of having created a group product. The science teacher was clear that with a new project in another class, he would do much more preparatory work with the students on how to work together in groups.

Example 3: Group work developing independence

Project title:	*Medieval realms*
Project focus:	Medieval England
Curriculum area:	History
Age group:	Year 7 (11–12 year olds)
Group structure:	Pairs, working on one computer for each pair
Location:	Computer room
Time:	One and a half hours a week for 5 weeks

This project was similarly structured to the previous example but was run in a girls' school with a strong tradition of group work. These students were in the middle of their first academic year in the school so had not yet had much experience but the ethos was apparent. The students all worked in pairs and were focused throughout the double lesson. Their history teacher described how the class worked together and how pairs helped other pairs, often asking each other for support: *'They came to realise that they were reliant on each other, came to take on that responsibility. When they finished they could facilitate others'.*

The students themselves saw their working together as very appealing, and certainly a starting point that they wanted to continue. Two girls discussing how they had worked together said:

Student 1: *It's been a lot more interesting. We've learned to work in pairs with a bit more independence, not relying on teachers all the time. We learned from our mistakes that we made.*
Student 2: *And we learned to work well with our partner and not just rely on her but do stuff ourselves.*
Student 1: *It makes you more reliable because if you don't do it, the whole project will be ruined 'cos you haven't done it. It makes you more reliable and independent.*
Student 2: *If you do this and people find out you can actually work together, then people ask you to do it again, and then you do it more often and it makes it easier.*

It is interesting that these students saw pair work as a way of moving from a reliance on the teacher to a reliance on each other, and that this gave them a sense of responsibility to their partner. Although the work was in pairs, both the students and the teacher felt that the work had given them a sense of independence, and that this was a positive aspect of their schoolwork.

At the end of this project each group's piece was linked up, but the teacher linked the work of different groups together into one piece and showed the whole group. Although the outcome was variable in quality, the class were really proud of their completed presentation and both class and teacher were enthusiastic about working in this way again.

These three examples from geography, history and science classes show how both collaboration and co-operation are useful, if not essential in multimedia authoring, however they are not simple to achieve. The examples show that learning to work in groups is a skill that needs to be learned, and needs to be taught, as the secondary science teacher explained: *'Teachers have to be multi-disciplinarians – as well as science, we need drama, art and the ability to manage groups'.*

In practice . . .

1. Whole class or small groups

In making this decision take into account how well you know the class, the students' experience of multimedia, and your own experience and confidence. Small groups are not necessarily easier than whole class work; planning and organisation are what make the projects run smoothly. However whole class work does need an overall structure, which is an extra aspect to consider. For a first project it is sensible to start small, and small groups rather than whole class work may be preferable.

In a *whole class project* the final product will be one interactive multimedia presentation contributed to by everyone. However there are a number of options.

- Whole class project where the class is involved in the whole idea from the outset and have a holistic sense of the piece with groups planning elements and pairs and individuals contributing to it. This way of working is shown in examples 1, 2 and 3. Although in these examples the initial idea was teacher imposed, the students knew where their work would be located and they had a sense of working together as a class. Of course students themselves could design the overall structure, but this may be fairly time consuming and they may have needed to have completed one project before they can understand what would be expected of them.
- Whole class project where the class is involved in the whole idea from the outset and have a sense of the piece but is worked on by individuals not groups. For example, consider the Tudor maze described in the introduction. The maze was a series of screens used as a structure for information to be tagged on to. The students designed paths going off in different directions with different links to information screens. This meant that the subject matter was limited to small one-screen size chunks and therefore too small for groups to work on. In this project, the class worked together in designing the whole piece and clarifying concepts around multimedia, indeed they became so skilled that they worked with other classes in the school showing them the software. However, in terms of content individual students worked on artwork and information for individual screens and then added this to the framework. Although this was a whole class project and the class certainly had a feeling of group authorship, students worked independently.
- Whole class project where the teacher has the overall structure in mind and the students simply contribute the elements to make the piece. For example, the teacher of the year-3 class (7–8 year olds) working on *Persephone* described in Chapter 2, had split the subject into four broad themes; the nature of history and time, the nature of facts and truth, the story of Persephone and characters' perspectives on the story. Although the class was nominally split into four groups to work on these themes, each individual worked on their own page of the story or piece of information about the Greeks which was later linked together by the teacher. Occasionally the students worked in pairs but again, although this was a whole class project and came together in its presentation, it was not essentially group work. In this project, the students were proud of the outcome, but had not had a sense of working together on a class piece as there was very little whole class work other than showing the piece at the end of some lessons.

In *small group projects* the final product will not be one class piece, as the outcome will be one complete presentation per group that will stand alone and not be linked to other pieces. In this model each group can be working on the same information, ideas and subject matter. They may work on different subjects but they will not need to consider how their work relates to others' work. The groups will complete the whole process from planning, to making, to evaluation as a small group, with some whole class teaching for multimedia concepts and computer skills, and working with another group for audience feedback.

For example, a class of 16–17 year olds working on debating were considering arguments around eating meat versus vegetarianism. Having watched a video and discussed the subject, the students split into pairs, each pair taking one side of the argument. Their task was to create a multimedia version of their argument in three linked screens. Their audience were the pairs working on the opposite side of the argument. This encouraged the students to seriously debate rather than 'advertise' their viewpoint. After two lessons, pairs looked at each others' work and discussed how convincing the presentations had been and why. In this example students were working on one of two aspects of the same subject, but repetition did not matter, indeed the different ways of producing the same facts were in fact the focus.

A multimedia project will end up with a number of different structures where learning and teaching take place:

- Whole class – initial brainstorming and planning of the large picture, direct teaching on issues of design, interactivity, audience and specific computer skills.
- Small groups – creating more detailed plans, storyboards and designs of their focused area, making decisions about what individual students or pairs will work on, giving feedback, technical help and sharing ideas.
- Pairs – working at the computer together, designing screens, writing text, making animations, adding sound, scanning images on to the computer and so on. It is hard to work with more than two at a computer screen, but two can be better than one.
- Individuals – creating artwork off the computer for screens and doing research for the information they need.

2. Co-operation or collaboration

Co-operation is important and will be a vital part of any multimedia authoring project, however, co-operative groups with their tight role-defined structure may be too prescriptive for multimedia authoring in the classroom. It will not work in terms of students learning all skills rather than only one or two, and in terms of National Curriculum access. Collaboration is particularly useful in developing creative ideas and is similarly important. There will be many opportunities in a multimedia authoring project for students to both co-operate and collaborate.

- *Co-operation* Working together at tables, sharing equipment, helping each other with drawing, teaching each other technical features on the computer and sharing skills.
- *Collaboration* Planning the work away from the computer, collecting information and designing screens, creating the work on the computer, developing ideas, learning to compromise and giving feedback.

3. Group skills

It is not simple to get groups to work well together. Living in a culture of competition, students often feel that criticism means being told off and the best way round this is to pass the buck to another member of the group. It is frustrating when asking a student why they have done something on the screen, positive or negative, for them to immediately respond with: *'It wasn't me, X did that'*. It is not only useful but vital to discuss with students the importance of group cohesion and make sure that ideas, group rules and criteria for assessing groups are all explicit from the start. I give my classes the maxim that if one member of the group has produced something good, then the whole group should take credit for it and if one member of the group is not pulling their weight, then the group should take that responsibility and share things out differently if necessary. This has meant that once when the scenario quoted above still happened, and my face showed its disappointment, the student in question immediately added in a bit of a chant, *'but I know, it's all our responsibility!'*

Students need to know what is expected of them in group work. Expectations help clarify and give students a structure to work in. This should include both the teacher's expectations of the group, and the team setting expectations for each other. The group essentially will be the main base for support and should be the first port of call before turning to the teacher. It may well be that some students already know certain skills or have picked them up quickly. Students can be encouraged to help each other whether or not they are in the same group. This could produce a cascade model in the classroom where students who have the skills assist students without them and these skills can continually be passed along. This may take some work as students are often not used to working together. Although some classrooms are set out in tables and students are used to sitting together to work, it is often still hard for them to work in groups. This is not a skill they have naturally but one that they will need to learn and practise. For co-operation students will need to learn to give and take, to be a cog in the wheel, not always working for their own individual needs. For collaboration, they will need to learn to listen to each other, contribute to the discussion and build on each others ideas. This requires practice. Exercises can be useful, for example:

- listening, and repeating what they have heard
- talking by referring to what the previous person has said
- thinking of ways or phrases to encourage other members of the group
- explaining something to someone without doing it for them
- setting up some group rules to be agreed by all group members.

Group rules will be particular to the class and it is important that they compose them because they are going to agree to abide by them. An example from one year-7 class (10–11 year olds) was that group members should:

- ask each other for help when they need it
- help someone when they ask for it
- encourage each other
- share ideas
- discuss things we don't like together
- be able to chat while we're working
- be loyal to each other.

The teacher might want to add some of his or her own rules, such as no mouse grabbing, and taking turns. No doubt the additional teacher rules could be negotiated.

4. Organising the activities

In a multimedia authoring classroom there are a number of activities that need to happen: discussion of concepts, planning, researching, collecting information, designing, drawing, scanning and linking. It is easier if the project is set up so that, at least at the beginning for discussion, planning and designing screens, students are working on the same activity at the same time. When they come to research and collect information they may well all be at different stages, and need to work both on and off the computer at different times.

5. Feedback

In this mixed activity classroom where individuals, pairs and groups are working on different aspects of the whole piece, it can be hard to keep the large picture in mind. Individuals and pairs should regularly share work with their group, and groups should present their work to the whole class (see Plate 3.2). In this way, although each student will be specialising, they will also get an overview of the whole subject, and although each student will be working on a small piece of the puzzle, they will get a sense of the whole presentation being authored.

Plate 3.2 Part of a group of students explaining to the class how their plan for their part of the project will work.

Each small group will be developing expertise in their area. For other students in the class to gain this knowledge too, there must be sharing between groups as well as within the group. Other groups may well be the best critics for each other as the project progresses.

Tips for multimedia groups

- Mixed ability groups work well in terms of sharing skills and helping each other.
- Do not work with more than six per group.
- Make sure groups are clear about what they are asked to do. A task sheet is a useful focus.
- It is easier if each group has the same task, even if the subject focus is different. It is then useful in the feedback session because the groups can learn from each other's ideas.
- Do not give groups more than one or a maximum of two things to do at the same time.
- Discuss and set group rules early and remind students of them frequently.
- Encourage help between groups rather than setting up a competitive element.

Checklist

- Decide whether the project will be a whole class project or small group project.
- Identify what tasks will use co-operation and collaboration.
- Identify who the groups are, taking into consideration gender, SEN and EAL, and consider mixed ability groupings.
- Decide what each group will be working on.
- Teach and discuss specific group skills.
- Discuss and produce group rules which can be hung on the walls and referred to.
- Design an initial task sheet or be clear about the first thing the groups will do.

Chapter 4

Space and time

Thinking about . . .

Space

Where should a multimedia authoring project take place? As a teacher you may not have a choice as the decision will be based on whether the school has a computer room that is available to be booked, or two machines at the side of the classroom; whether the machines have the correct software installed, and how many are working at any one time. A school decision regarding computer location will have already been made based on network capability, convenience, security, finance and structure of the school building and classrooms as well as on an educational theory of computers in schools. The theory leading to where computers are located is important because it makes a statement about the role of technology in the curriculum. Decisions about computer *use* follow from decisions about location, and this affects the atmosphere of a project. Computer location, therefore is dependent on how computers are viewed in the school.

Computers can be seen in different ways, from a glorified typewriter to a number cruncher, from an integrated learning system to a panacea of educational problems, from a communication device to an encyclopaedia, from a mixed toolkit to a scary box of metal and chips in the corner. The computer can be seen as complete in itself and the major focus of attention, or as one individual tool or simply as the paper to write on.

If the computer is seen as the focus where all the work takes place, then nothing else apart from the technology itself is needed to do the ICT work. From the machine the student can write, draw, solve problems, research, fax and e-mail. It has revolutionised our access to information and our ability to communicate quickly across distances. From this perspective a networked computer room would be ideal because skills can be taught in a skills session where all students are learning together to become independent users of the technology. If the computer is seen as a tool, however, such as a crayon to draw with, then it is only one tool among many, and choosing to use this particular tool rather than any other will be because it is the best piece of equipment to perform a particular function. This follows that it may not always be the best tool, and crayons themselves may be better at times. In this case the computer needs to be as accessible as the pencils, pens and paints. This accessibility may be in the guise of a networked computer at the side of the classroom or it may involve thinking about creating computer *class*rooms rather than simply computer rooms. The computer can also be seen as a piece of paper, that is the container for information from other sources. Just as paper can be written on or drawn on, and can hold ideas, so the computer can do the same. Similarly in this situation, access to a computer when needed will be paramount, and having to book a room will mean that the computer cannot be used spontaneously. These views of what computers are for are not mutually exclusive, and indeed computers are usually used for more than one function as schools might have both computer rooms and computers in classrooms, however one theoretical perspective will often predominate.

In cross curriculum multimedia authoring projects the computer is used as a tool. Multimedia and web authoring software are simply structures or containers to hold the information the students put into them. Information may be accessed on the computer but this is only one place where students can research. Much of the work in a multimedia authoring project happens off the computer, such as planning, research from books, painting or creating images for scanning, interviewing, taking photographs or video. The computer will become the medium for collating and presenting ideas. Given that a multimedia authoring project happens on many fronts, the ideal location would be one where there is space to work both on and off the computer as the need arises. This does not imply that there is a perfect location for a multimedia authoring project; often the location will not be completely right and there will need to be some flexible thought around the use of available space. Quality work can be done in all kinds of situations. For example, *The Moon* was a multimedia project authored by four students using two old and slow computers at the side of a small crowded classroom/hut in the playground. There was constant noise and activity with students having to squeeze past the computers to move around the room. Despite these obstacles the piece came runner up in the European Multimedia Awards in 1997. This example is certainly not to advocate using old equipment in less than ideal circumstances, but is to suggest that it is not necessary to wait for the conditions to be perfect.

Computer locations

1. Computer rooms

Computer rooms vary considerably. They can simply be a room full of computers (Figure 4.1) or they can be creative workshops (Figure 4.2). If a computer room only has computers and IT equipment in it with no space for anything else, then of course, that will be the primary focus because the students will be coming there to do computers, and that will be seen as the main attraction even if it is a part of their science or

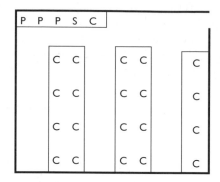

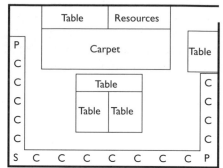

Figure 4.1 A computer room.   *Figure 4.2* A creative workshop.

C = computer, S = scanner, P = printer

(The carpet is an area where primary school students sit together to listen and have discussions.)

geography lesson. If a computer room is a creative workshop with tables to work on and access to pens and crayons, paper and books, then students can choose when to use the computer and when to work away from it. It will be more like a classroom with 15 computers in it. This will help to view the project as an integrated piece of classroom curriculum work.

Example 1: Computer workshop

One small primary school had a newly built computer room of 15 Apple Mac machines connected to the Internet. It was set up like a classroom with a carpeted area so that students could sit on the floor, tables in the centre, and space for resources such as paper, pens and books. During a multimedia authoring project on electricity, students working in groups or pairs used all the available space. On one afternoon while one group was sitting on the floor reworking their plan, students from other groups were creating artwork at the tables. Some students were researching in books and posters while two others were finding information on the Internet. There were students scanning work and others were designing screens and linking them together at the computer. It felt very similar to a regular classroom project where there were multiple activities, and the computer was there to be used, but not all the time. Plates 4.1 and 4.2 show a computer workshop, and students at work.

Example 2: Small computer workshop

Another primary school in the borough moved all of their classroom computers into one room. This made a room of eight computers with printers, a scanner, a dial-up line for Internet access and tables in the centre. This would have been ideal except for the fact that there were always one or two computers or printers that needed fixing, and the room was not quite big enough for a whole class to be comfortably working there. When working on a multimedia authoring project, classes had to be split into two groups, some working on artwork and research in the classroom while others worked on the computers in the computer workshop. The obvious problem was that for any computer project, the class needed two teachers.

Plates 4.1 and 4.2 Computer workshops allow work to be done on and off the computers as appropriate.

2. Computers in classrooms

Computers in classrooms can be organised in different ways. Where the computers are placed in a classroom is dependent on where the power points or network sockets are, away from a sink and where they will not get splashed with paint. One machine can be tucked away in a corner isolated from other things so that it is not seen as central and when used it is something apart from the regular classroom (Figure 4.4). It may be less

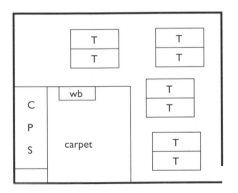
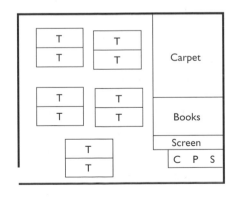

Figure 4.3 A classroom with a computer in an ideal position for whole class teaching.

Figure 4.4 A classroom with the computer tucked away behind a screen.

Key: C = computer, S = scanner, P = printer, T = table, wb = white board distracting for other students but it also sends a message that working on the computer is special and different. On the other hand the computer can be strategically placed so that it is ready to use when needed and in a good position for displaying and teaching the whole class (see Figure 4.3 and Plate 4.3).

Some classrooms have pods of three or four computers (Figure 4.5). This sets up the possibility of using the computer as it is needed as a reference tool while still leaving other computers free for different work. This is a good mid-way option between a computer workshop and an integrated classroom computer.

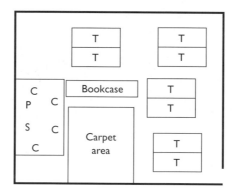

Figure 4.5 A classroom with a pod of four computers.

Example 3: Integrated classroom computer

One classroom of a small primary school has the computer beside the carpeted area where students sit for whole class teaching. On one side is a white board, on the other side is the computer. The teacher, sitting in the middle, uses both to teach with and display information. In two half-hour sessions per week, she teaches IT skills which are then practised during the week as a part of the project. The computer has a scanner attached and leads running from it for a digital camera and for a portable word processor. This gives students the opportunity to create artwork, take photographs and write text off the computer and use the computer as a way of drawing all this information together in an interactive multimedia framework. The outcome of multimedia projects run in this classroom is a computer presentation, wall displays and large folders of students' work. The classroom teacher described the availability of the computer as affecting the way students think about presenting work. She gave an example of a class journey to a residential centre in the country. On their return the students were full of ideas as to how they could present what they had learned through multimedia authoring. The teacher explained: '*they make the links because the computer's there and they get used to using it in that integrated way in different subjects*'.

Plate 4.3 Integrated classroom where the computer is well positioned for whole class teaching.

3. Mobile computers

There are situations where there are not enough computers in a school for every class to have one, and there is not enough space for a computer room. Computers in some schools are put on trolleys and wheeled into rooms when they are needed. The advantage of this is that the computers come into the regular classroom. The disadvantage is that they will be seen as special rather than commonplace, and may be used less often. On the other hand using laptop computers can be very versatile. Small cheap laptops can be taken on field trips to use for research, can be brought into the classroom on students' desks and can be shared between classes.

Example 4: Computers on trolleys

In the science department of a secondary school in Hackney there are five science labs which do not have computers permanently in place. Instead there are six computers that can be brought into the labs on trolleys. In a multimedia authoring project on the Periodic Table, two computers were wheeled into the science lab for the project. Although this could have integrated the computers into the class work, it did not. The computers were used as a way of revising and extending chemistry work that had already been done. This meant that the students working on the project were missing the class lab lesson and needed to catch up on it later. As there were only four students working on the computers during each lesson this was not a big difficulty, but was also not a good solution to integrating the ICT.

Example 5: Laptops in the classroom

Another secondary school in the borough has a single computer at the side of the classroom and supplements this by using laptops. This worked well in a multimedia authoring project in history as the laptops became a mobile tool in the classroom, and all the usual classroom resources were still available. However there can be difficulties. The laptops in this school are shared with other classes and with teachers who can take them home for their own use. This means that the laptops need to be booked by the subject teacher, then brought in by other teachers who have not fully charged the batteries. They can run from the mains, but an English teacher wanting to use the laptops without enough sockets in her classroom needs to change rooms and rearrange the furniture in the other room so that the tables are all near a socket, not leaving many tables to work on away from the computers. Essentially, using the laptops in an English project on narrative worked very well, however, there was a lot of energy expended on logistics.

Multimedia authoring can take place in any of these situations, but the most successful projects will be located in a classroom or a computer workshop large enough to fit the whole class, where the computer is only used as and when it is needed giving the project work space and flexibility.

Time

There seems to be some teacher anxiety that multimedia authoring projects take up too much time to fit into the curriculum. It may indeed be true that it takes more time to do a multimedia authoring geography project using computers than teaching the same material with traditional methods, however the benefits of extending the amount of time to include the computer work are substantial. The students will be learning computer skills and concepts at the same time as learning the subject, but the hope is that the enthusiasm students bring to computer work will also be linked to the subject matter. The additional time can be accommodated if planned in advance. As computers generally become more integrated in schools, students will become more skilled and teachers more confident in the process, so that multimedia authoring will become one of the repertoire of standard ways of presenting curriculum work and this greater familiarity will make it more contained. A first time project is an investment because it will be a learning ground for the teacher as well as the students and will take longer than subsequent projects which will be easier to manage timewise.

In practice . . .

It is important to take advantage of whatever space you have to work in. As suggested, the project works best if the space includes both computers and tables or desks to work at away from the computers.

Integrated computer classroom

In a one computer classroom, the multimedia authoring work can be integrated with the project work happening both on and off the computer – some students researching or producing artwork to be scanned in, while others create computer animation or link screens. In this situation, many activities will be happening concurrently in the classroom, all geared towards the presentation, with work building up slowly during the life of the project. The plans can be pinned up on the walls so that students can refer to them and tick off screens as they are completed. It is useful to have portable text processors so that some of the students can be writing text away from the computer. The project will need to be given some concentrated time at the beginning for students to produce the data, but it will slow down as the designs are completed off the computer and students need to continue the work at the screen. The project work will have to change from having the whole class working on the project at the same time to students working in turns at the computer. This works particularly well in primary schools where the computer input can be more flexible, using available time throughout the week. For both primary and secondary schools, students will need some ICT skills input. In a school that has a computer room as well as computers in classrooms, it may be useful to have one session all together to learn the software. Otherwise one or two skills at a time should be demonstrated to the class, letting students take turns to practise them during the week. There will also need to be time set aside for discussion of different aspects of multimedia such as audience, structure, interactivity and design issues (these will be looked at in the next few chapters), as well as considering how the subject matter itself relates to these multimedia issues. These discussions should come fairly early on but should be reviewed throughout the project as students' technical abilities and conceptual understanding develop.

Creative computer workshop

Working in a computer room each group or pair will have their own computer to work on. The lure of computers is strong enough to keep students at the computer for all the available time, so they will need to be reminded that much of the work will happen off the computer. It is a good idea to have one computer lesson to learn skills, then two lessons in the classroom for planning, designing and creating artwork, before going back to the computer room. Alternatively the project could be structured so that there is a classroom-based lesson for direct teaching, with research time in between each computer room class. It is also possible for the students to do research while they are working in the computer room from CD ROMs, the Internet and books brought in for this purpose. If the multimedia project is a re-presentation of work students have already completed in class, their planning will need to be rigorous, but this will cut down the time needed at the computers.

In a whole class project, each group's computer will end up with a part of the complete presentation which will need to be linked to other groups' work. All the different stacks and files will need to be copied on to one computer or saved into one area in the network. This can be assigned to a group who have the role of linking the different pieces, making an introduction, title and contents page. As a teacher, you may choose to do this yourself as a way of keeping your multimedia authoring skills on a par with the rest of the class.

Suggested timetable for a multimedia authoring project

Class 1: *(take a class to be approximately a one hour lesson)*

Examine and analyse examples of other students' multimedia presentations considering non-linear structure and interactivity (examples that can be used are on the CD ROM).

Look at the material to be studied explaining themes you may have predefined.

Discuss overall structure.

Class 2: *(only if the class is unfamiliar with the software)*

Introduction to the software. Play to get a sense of how the program works. (For a one-computer-classroom project this will need to be demonstrated a few times together, but individuals will need to practice at other times during the week.)

Class 3: *(in a classroom you may want to wait until all students have seen the software)*

Discuss the purpose of the piece and who the audience will be.

Assign groups and topics.

Design group plans including navigation routes and interactive elements.

Begin sketching individual screens.

Give feedback to whole group.

Next X classes: *(X is the length of time you want to spend on the project. In a one-computer classroom, this time may need to be flexible during the week)*

Work on the presentation, adding content as text, graphics, sound and link the screens together.

Create artwork off the computer and scan in.

Informally show pieces to other class members for ongoing feedback.

Second to last class:

Link up the pieces on the computer. Review it as a whole class.

Show the first draft of the finished pieces to a sample audience, discuss and act on any ideas received.

Last class: Finish off and evaluate the work.

Space and time tips

- It is useful if students know where their space is, each group having a project table, each pair having a project computer.
- Arrange the room so that resources are well placed for use when the students need them. This may entail taking classroom paper, pens, etc. into the computer room.
- Start small, smaller than you think you can manage.
- Students will start slowly. In four one-hour sessions for a first project, limit them to two or three screens, so that they have time to plan and finish well. For later projects they should get through one or two screens per lesson. Remind students that good screens with interesting content and graphics are a pleasure. Three of these are better than six shoddy ones.
- For a first project limit animation, video and fancy effects because they take time to learn. These are better suited to project number two.
- Ensure that the same issues discussed at the beginning (audience, design, interactivity) are constant themes under review in each lesson.

Checklist

- Have a look at the software before the project begins.
- Book the computer room or locate where the computers are.
- Create enough space around the computers for research and artwork.
- Check the software is up and running on the computers.
- Split the curriculum content up into pair or group sized chunks.
- Work out how many classes are needed and add one for contingencies.
- Be realistic about how much the students can do in the time allocated.
- Give yourself enough time at the end to do any finishing off that is necessary.

Chapter 5

Audience

Thinking about . . .

We are all used to be being an audience for multimedia whether it is television, theatre, CD ROM or the Internet. We make judgements and choices about what we like and what we do not like, what is interesting and what is useful, what we find hard to watch or difficult to use, what makes us laugh, what bores us and what makes us think we could do better. This experience of being a consumer of others' creativity makes us all potential experts and the hours that students have put into watching television or playing computer games can be used as a starting point in the classroom and as a source of motivation for students presenting their own multimedia curriculum work. Expertise can be developed by students becoming a more critical audience, assessing the value of existing familiar media. This first step, evaluating what works for an audience will be essential information for them to take into consideration when making their own multimedia piece. The students may be used to being an audience, but they need direction in developing critical expertise so that they can distinguish between effective and non-effective multimedia. From themselves being the audience, they now need to see the audience as another person.

When students explain an idea to someone else they need to think about the subject matter not just in terms of how well they understand it themselves, but how well they can communicate it to the other person. In order to do this, they have to analyse their own learning process, taking note of what helps them to learn. Harel and Papert (1990) say that by designing software in logo (a programming language), the students were 'thinking about their own thinking' (p. 5). However, rather than just generalising from their own experience of learning, they must also consider the particular audience they have in mind and try to find the best way of helping them to understand the information they are putting across. Lafer (1996) argues that 'the ability and desire to understand the thoughts of others are essential to the development of critical thinking ability' (p. 145). The 'internalization of audience' asks students to compare their own thoughts with thoughts of other people, which helps them to create meaning. Although students may use their own learning as a model, Williams (1998) claims they still need to 'make guesses about what will amuse, please, inform, educate, puzzle, enthral, excite, stimulate, reward their audiences'. These guesses, however can be informed ones and will be part of 'building a system that encapsulates that [their own] model' (p. 158).

There are many possible audiences for students' multimedia work. This needs to be considered in advance as the decision will affect how the piece is presented. Usually in the classroom the teacher is the sole audience for students' work. The teacher is such a familiar audience to the students that they may not consider him or her an 'audience' at all. This could mean that students are less careful to ensure that each screen 'makes sense' or is correctly linked up, because if it does not work properly, it is not a disaster as it is 'only for the teacher'. Students may feel that it is less important to be succinct and clear about what they mean, assuming that the teacher can fill in the gaps (as well as correcting their spelling, punctuation and grammar). Of course, you as teacher will always be an audience to the students' work and will want to use the final piece as a part of assessing the project, however, you will be an additional audience, not the sole one.

Apart from the teacher the most common audience for schoolwork is the rest of the class. Students share work with their table, read out work to the whole class, give and get feedback from a partner, work in groups and display work on the walls. Work on display however has a wider audience of parents or other students and teachers who come into the classroom. These additional audiences will give a different sort of feedback to the authors which is not about assessment or getting right and wrong answers, and more about what they like the look of and how they feel about it. Using an audience for testing a piece and giving important critical feedback will be explored in more detail in Chapter 10.

In multimedia authoring it is possible for the presentation to get out of the classroom into the wider sphere of the whole school or the outside world of other schools, a local museum or the Internet. Whatever the situation the important element is that the students get a sense of writing for a real live audience. The more real the audience and the more real the purpose for doing the piece, the more real the task will be for the students and the more focused they will be in making an appropriate presentation. McGrath *et al.* (1997) suggest that students using multimedia authoring to demonstrate their learning to a real audience 'should help improve (a) the attitude with which students approach their work, (b) the quality of their work, and (c) their senses of ownership of that work' (p. 20).

A real audience can be known, such as students in the class next door or parents at a parents' evening. The audience can be mixed, such as students of different ages, or both parents and students. It can be partially unknown, such as people who walk into a museum or gallery or it can be completely unknown, such as a website. If the audience is completely unknown it may be difficult to direct the presentation, so only a part of that audience might be taken into account when making the piece. Who the audience is can be seen as a continuum. At one end is the teacher, where students do not need to think about audience any more than in their regular work, and can use a shorthand and hope it will be understood. At the other end is an audience of different ages and needs and where clarity and differentiation will be paramount. This continuum is shown in Figure 5.1

The audience (or users) are a crucial factor that will need to be accommodated, and targeting the piece towards different groupings will require a different way of thinking about the multimedia presentation. If the audience is known the piece can be made personal to them. Many student multimedia presentations are made as curriculum materials for a younger age group specifically because it will encourage the students to think about how to explain difficult concepts as clearly and succinctly as possible. Secondary age students making materials on a scientific topic for primary age students

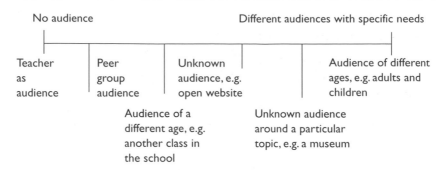

Figure 5.1 Continuum showing a progression of complexity in the nature of an audience.

will need to make sure that they do not assume an amount of knowledge, that they detail their ideas step by step, and that they write it in language that is understandable, explaining any jargon they use.

If the audience is mixed, students may want to offer different options to the user by making screens at different levels of understanding or making sure that on each screen the information is communicated in various ways, including having the text read out. If the audience is unknown, they will need to direct the work to an average user or simply make it as clear and understandable as possible. A year 10 technology class (14 and 15 year olds) made a presentation on different types of materials for primary students. They had a title screen which read, *'Hello Blods and Blodwins'*, and used language such as, *'You have entered the EBONY ZONE'*. When asked why they wrote it in that way, one of the boys responded that it would make kids want to read it.

A school in America situated inside a zoo made an interactive zoo guide with animal facts which was then used at the zoo visitors' centre. This study by Beichner (1994) showed the students' concern for clarity of information in text, pictures and navigation. The final piece needed to be easily understandable, clearly labelled and useful so that the audience would want to use it and be encouraged to see and find out about the animals, and know how to 'play' it without complex instructions. Accuracy was extremely important and this was motivated by the students' awareness that their classroom work had direct application outside the classroom. Beichner describes how the students went over and over a video sequence to be absolutely certain that the information they were going to use was correct. An interesting aspect of this project was that after the project was completed, the students in this school could watch visitors, both adults and children, using their presentation. The real world use of their piece was utterly explicit. The students could see clearly whether technical aspects such as navigation worked or not, but could also get a sense of how visitors actually used the piece, in this case spending only small amounts of time looking at tiny portions and ignoring most of it. There is an important lesson these students must have learned, that as authors they had to let the piece go out of their hands to stand on its own for the visitors to use, without any prodding direction to look at their favourite screens.

Example 1: Awareness of audience

Project title: *Evolution and inheritance*
Project focus: Darwin, Mendel, cell division, inheritance and DNA
Curriculum area: Science
Age group: Year 10 (14–15 year olds)
Group structure: Pairs working on different aspects of the whole piece
Location: Computer room
Time: 9 × 50 minute sessions
Audience: Top primary and early secondary (9–14 year olds)

To begin the project students were shown animated multimedia science work from students in years 5–11. They had two reactions to seeing the work. First, the students were impressed with the medium, the sound, the moving between screens and the humour that came across, and were eager to do something similar themselves. Second, as they laughed at some of the childish images drawn straight on the computer with the mouse, they said, *'that's rubbish, we could do better than that'*. Both these responses came from students' experience of what multimedia should and could look like, and both responses contributed to the enthusiasm of these students to make their own multimedia adventure games.

The class were split into pairs, each working on a separate aspect of the final piece, creating their own interactive elements and design of between three and ten screens. Some of the class had used multimedia before in their ICT lessons and for some it was entirely new, however none of the class had ever made their own multimedia programs before. The concept of audience was discussed briefly at the beginning of the project where students were told that their work would go on to a CD ROM for top primary and lower secondary classes in Hackney. The class brainstormed what they thought needed to be taken into consideration for explaining ideas to students of this age. Towards the end of the project the students talked about what were the important things to think about when making the piece for a particular audience.

Two girls working on Mendel explained:

> *You have to make sure it goes with the sort of people you want it for. If you do it for older people and it's too babyish then older people will find it too babyish. If it's for younger people and it's too old, they won't understand it.*

This pair had made a collage of peas that they had scanned into the computer as a background and a line drawing of Mendel had also been scanned in. The girl who had done the pictures explained how important it was to use illustrations and diagrams so that younger children *'wouldn't get bored and go on to something else'*; although some of the class wanted to use computer clip-art which was fairly devoid of character. The girl who had drawn the peas had clear views on this

Student 1:   *Your own pictures are better than those from a book, they're more interesting for children, not like clipart.*

Student 2:   *Yea, and like those football pictures [the boys in the class had been using].*

Student 1:   *'Cos you've got to make it interesting for girls as well as boys.*

These comments show an awareness of audience difference and the need to take gender into account as well as age.

Another two girls working on pairing chromosomes transferred carefully planned text and pictures from paper to the screen. The screen contained diagrams of the chromosomes with minimal writing (see Screen shot 5.1). One of the girls explained:

> *When I'm explaining it I have to have in mind I'm making it for younger children so I have to make it interesting, not too much writing, a lot of pictures to show what I'm talking about and make it clearer.*

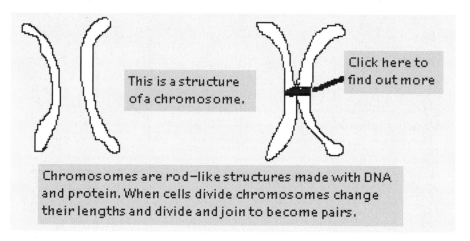

This is a structure of a chromosome.

Click here to find out more

Chromosomes are rod-like structures made with DNA and protein. When cells divide chromosomes change their lengths and divide and join to become pairs.

Screen shot 5.1 Using small chunks of writing to explain concepts means condensing the information into a couple of sentences.

These students saw the importance of using *'bits of writing'* rather than long sections of text. Although this could be seen cynically as an excuse not to do much writing, in fact the students had to work very hard to condense the large amounts of information they wanted to convey into a short but clear summary identifying the most important points. The girl describing how she accommodated the audience also admitted that when she got involved in the nuts and bolts of making the piece she forgot who she was making it for and just got on with it, and later needed to check back that it was clear enough.

Two boys were creating a 'zoom in' on a cell, starting with a picture of a person and getting smaller and smaller. They had set it up so that at a click the user would move to the next size down. One of them described it as a *'puzzle'* because *'it can be fun to learn. They [the audience] get entertained, maybe a bit of education and ideas, so they can do something like this'.* They had researched the information from scratch in order to create the piece, and saw their own clear understanding of the subject as essential:

Student 1:   *If you couldn't understand it, they [the audience] couldn't – you've got to make it simple.*

Student 2:   *If you're confused, then they'll be confused.*

This pair began with a title page full of bright colours on a zig zag background (see Screen shot 5.2). They explained:

Student 2:   *You have to make it groovy and funky so it looks interesting. If you had 'zoom in on a cell' on a white background it'd be boring – with this background, they won't be able to believe their eyes.*

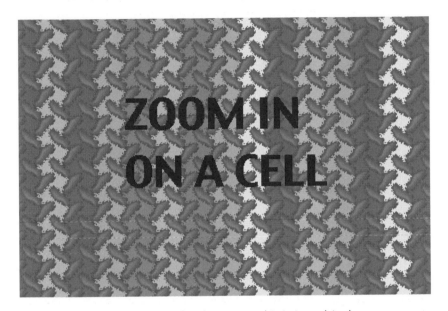

Screen shot 5.2 Title screen. On the screen this is in multicolour.

However, after feedback from other members of the class who objected to the computer generated patterns, these two changed their title screen to something simpler with a blue background. Without checking for feedback this time they added a computer generated animation of a frog jumping, which had nothing to do with their piece. One of the boys explained:

Student 2:   *If you don't have anything fun on it, no one will want to read it.*

The awareness of audience in this class came across in a number of different ways from simple language to using colour. One pair set up their piece as a cartoon of a teacher explaining dominant and recessive genes to a brother and sister. Other pairs used an interactive format where the user had to click on the objects to find out how many chromosomes they contained. This type of interactivity will be looked at in more detail in Chapter 8.

Example 2: Difficulties in conceptualising audience

Project title:	*Petsy*
Project focus:	Stories
Curriculum area:	Literacy
Age group:	Year 2 (age 6–7)
Group structure:	Whole class, pairs and individual work
Location:	One computer at the side of the classroom
Time:	One morning a week for 6 weeks
Audience:	BBC Education website for early years (3–5 year olds)

A year-2 class (6 and 7 year olds) made a multimedia story presentation around literacy work inspired by the BBC's 'Words and Pictures' series of programmes. They were told that the final piece was to go on the BBC Education website, to be used by a younger age group. However, they found it difficult to keep audience on the Internet in mind as they made their piece. Some of them knew what the Internet was but most were not familiar with it. Their teacher talked about how they associated the BBC with television, thought the BBC would interview them and that they would be on the news that night. Indeed when they heard that two people from the BBC Education website were coming in to see their work and talk to them, they assumed that this meant 'Blue Peter' presenters. The idea of a website went over their heads. Even though the understanding of such an abstract audience was too difficult for students of this age, the word BBC was enough to motivate and excite them. This project is described in more detail in Chapter 13.

Example 3: Thinking about learning

Project title:	*Rainforests*
Project focus:	People, insects, animals and climate of a rainforest
Curriculum area:	Geography/Science
Age group:	Year 6 (10 and 11 year olds)
Group structure:	Whole class, pairs and individual work
Location:	One computer at the side of the classroom
Time:	Over a 5-week period
Audience:	Year 3 (7–8 year olds) in their school

This class were told that their task was to teach younger students about rainforests. The teacher began by asking her students to consider the process they themselves went through in the classroom when they learned something. The class discussed this and came out with the rather simplified version of how first they were given information and then they were tested to see if they knew it. She then asked them what helped them to learn and quoted the class as saying to her, *'what we find in maths is when we do mental maths and you make it into a game then we learn about it quicker, and we want to do it again'.* This was a useful opener to considering the sort of things 7- and 8-year-old children would enjoy doing on the computer because if they could make their presentation into a game for their audience, they would *'learn about it quicker'.*

At the end of every project session there was feedback time where the class looked at each other's work on the computer. On a number of occasions a younger student from the school came to that session and tried out the work they had been doing. The class then discussed what they noticed. There were two major responses that the students found. First, 7 and 8 year olds do not all read very well, so they needed to simplify text for them and use less of it, adding voice-overs more often. Second, the younger students needed something to 'do', not just sit there and look at the screen, so the class made many interactive sequencing games and quizzes (see Chapter 8). One group working on climate in the rainforests felt that they could not simplify what they wanted to say enough to make it understandable by young students. This group eventually decided, with the agreement of their teacher, to change this theme.

The teacher said that she was amazed at the way the students were articulating their own experience of learning and considering that experience as a way of thinking about how to teach something to others. She stressed that this was unusual and related their motivation to the fact that most of their work is done only for her, but this work was going beyond her to outsiders.

In these examples older students showed an understanding of creating something for someone else and this awareness made them take time to consider appropriate images and text. The year-10 class felt simplicity, pictures and fun were important to engage younger students, and making complex concepts in genetics more simple was not an easy task. The year-6 class, who had done a number of multimedia authoring projects before and were already fairly sophisticated authors, felt that audience interactivity was important and most of their pieces included animations, sound and dragging objects. Although they were making it for year 3, the year-6 class themselves enjoyed playing these interactive games, showing how they had based these ideas on their own preferences for learning. The year-2 class did not have a sense of audience as they were focused on the here and now, which was writing the story. Younger students often do what they are asked to by their teachers simply because they are asked to do so, whereas for older students, doing things without a clear purpose can seem pointless, and an audience can provide this purpose.

In practice . . .

1. Begin considering audience in general

Students need to get a sense of how multimedia is aimed at particular audiences. This might not be something they have considered before in great detail. A useful starting point is to analyse other multimedia pieces, both commercial and students' work, and think about who they are designed for, answering the following questions.

- Who is the program aimed at?
- How can you tell?
- Is it a wide or narrow range of people?
- Do you agree on the audience the program makers say they are addressing?
- What would you need to change about the piece if the audience was different?

These are not necessarily easy questions to answer, but it will serve to focus the students' minds towards the questions they will need to ask themselves about their own multimedia presentation. Students may find that they want to direct their piece to a similar audience to that of the work they have seen, and can glean ideas from these examples, or they may find that they want to do something very different from what they have seen and need to think afresh.

2. Decide on the purpose

The first consideration is one of purpose. Multimedia authoring is being used for a reason, and that reason needs to be clear. Working without knowing 'why' will make it difficult to choose what information to use, so having a clear objective is important. The narrow purpose may be defined by the subject matter, which is to present information in order to, for example:

- explain the causes of the First World War
- describe what life was like in medieval England
- retell a well known fairy tale
- explore how blood circulation works in the human body.

The content could be about anything in the curriculum where there is information in the form of facts, ideas, stories or opinions to be transmitted. Information, however, is not objective, and students will present their version with their particular point of view, expressed in a way that is meaningful to them. They will probably need to start studying the subject to know their point of view, and they may want to decide a class line so their whole piece has some consistency, or they may choose to put across all their individual and different viewpoints. There will also be a broader purpose underlying the content; this may be to teach, entertain, test, show, tell, convince or any combination of these.

3. Decide who the audience is

The decision about audience needs to be taken at the beginning of the project but it does not necessarily need to be taken by the students. As a teacher you might want to make this decision yourself. For a first project it is easier to start small and with a known audience of peers or another class in the school. Later projects can include local galleries, museums and libraries who are often happy to display school students' work either on their website or on a computer in the building. These local organisations might have education officers who can visit the school and work with the project. Bringing the outside world into the classroom with the students, will give them a sense of their work being real, and important enough to go public. There may even be funding available from these quarters.

4. Discuss factors that need to be taken into consideration

When the purpose and audience have been decided, it will bring into play a number of factors. Class discussion and thought need to go into making the piece engaging for the audience, so that:

- the wording matches the level of understanding of the audience
- the sound and pictures are age appropriate
- the information is as accurate as possible
- it includes an element of humour or personality
- it is clear how to navigate the piece
- it includes interactivity on the screen to give the audience both something to do and something to think about.

If the purpose is to teach about the subject, the students will need to make the information clear, simple and easy to understand. If the purpose is to entertain, the students may want to use humour, puzzles and lots of interactivity. If the purpose is to test, the students will need to design games and quizzes where there are right and wrong answers. If the purpose is to convince, they will have to carefully construct a good argument. In all cases students will need to consider design.

Audience tips

- The clearer the purpose, the easier it is for students to collect relevant data.
- Make sure students share their ideas often, as finding out new things when collecting data can change their ideas and change what they want to say.
- A particular audience familiar to the students is easier to start with than multiple or unknown audiences.
- For a second project, getting outside agencies involved can increase both motivation and the care that students put into their work.
- Remind students regularly of the purpose and audience as they are working.

Checklist

- Analyse work by other students and commercial software with audience in mind.
- Decide on the purpose of the piece.
- Decide on audience.
- Consider how the purpose will relate to how they will structure the piece.
- Consider what features are important in accommodating the audience.

Chapter 6

Designing screens

Thinking about . . .

Authoring multimedia in the classroom is a creative act. It takes raw materials such as paper, paints, pencils and computers, information and ideas and, using the catalyst of imagination, turns it into an interactive multimedia presentation of images, text, animation, sound and video. Multimedia is not a book where text is the key element holding all the information and putting concepts into a form of words. It is not a piece of artwork where a perceived or imagined idea is turned into an image or visual representation. It is not a radio broadcast where sound effects and language describe the scene and tell the story. Multimedia is a combination, more similar to film or television, where there is the opportunity to create an interactive presentation where no one medium is key. The most successful multimedia presentations are pieces where the image tells a part of the story, the text tells more and the sound adds something else, not repeating each other, but adding up to a whole experience of meaning. We can see this as the difference between annotated text and integrated composition (Hay *et al.* 1994).

Annotated text

In annotated text, as shown in Screen shots 6.1 and 6.2, the pictures, animation and sound simply accompany or annotate the text. The text provides all the information needed to understand the piece, and the non-textual elements illustrate it. If you remove

Screen shots 6.1 and 6.2 Examples of annotated text. The text holds all the information; the pictures illustrate but do not add extra information. The sound reads the text.

the pictures or the sound, you would not destroy the meaning because it is contained in the text.

Integrated composition

In integrated composition, the individual media are integrated parts of the whole meaning. The picture may give a background to the meaning, the text adds another element, the sound moves the story on and the animation explains the process. Here if you remove the sound or the picture, the piece cannot be understood because the meaning is contained in the combined effect of the media used. Examples of integrated composition are shown in Screen shots 6.3 and 6.4.

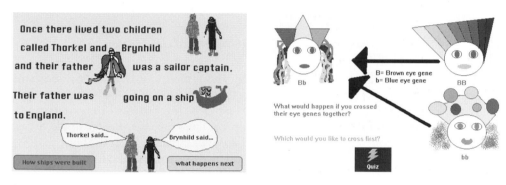

Screen shots 6.3 and 6.4 Examples of integrated composition. In both these cases taking away one medium would destroy the meaning.

The strength of integrated composition is in giving students the opportunity to express the same idea in many different but *simultaneous* ways. If each of the different media is seen as different sections of an orchestra, each section has its own part, but they need to play together for the piece of music to sound like a complete ensemble, as the piece was written.

This can be seen as a continuum, as shown in Figure 6.1, with annotated text at one end and integrated composition at the other. Different ages and different contexts may require different points on this continuum. Younger children will find illustrated stories easier to make as they can concentrate on creating the meaning in one medium (text) and then adding to this meaning in a second medium (pictures). On the integrated composition end the thought processes are much more complex, as the student needs to consider which media are the best ways of transmitting meaning, and how this meaning is embedded in the mixture of media.

Although students create integrated compositions it is difficult to describe the whole multimedia piece without referring to individual elements. Our society's organisation and the structure of our language demand that when we speak we split up concepts, and so in explaining creative pieces of work it is easier to think of things by splitting them up. Although this may have to be done, it is important to be aware that splitting up can put undue emphasis on one medium and that this will distort the true picture. It is important to keep in mind that describing experience is only an approximation of the experience itself. Wittgenstein wrote that the limits of language are not the limits

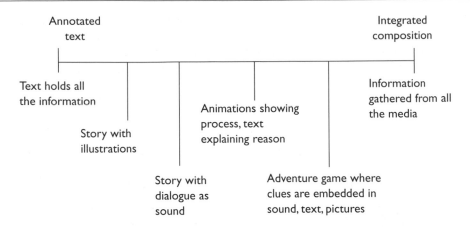

Figure 6.1 A continuum of annotated text to integrated composition.

of reality, but are the limits of what we can say about reality. It is difficult to describe holistic concepts because language tends to compartmentalise and structure ideas. This needs to be taken into account when students describe the process of creating multimedia presentations – they struggle to find appropriate language. For example, when year-5 students (9 and 10 year olds) were asked what they enjoyed about making multimedia games (see Example 1 in this chapter), their responses all referred to discrete areas – drawing, writing, sound, animation and so on, most choosing two or three different media. Indeed, as they started saying what they enjoyed, they went through most of what they had done. Four students struggling to explain the use of multimedia described how it worked in a different way to a book:

Student 1: *You don't have to stay in one thing all the time. You can choose different things.*
Student 2: *We got to try out different things how to do a story . . . It's not a straightforward story. You just write different things in it, like animation and sound effects and it's moving. It's different.*
Student 3: *In books you don't get animals that talk.*
Student 4: *It makes sound. It makes books sound.*

This new medium contains new concepts and therefore needs new words to fit the job, and these are only in the process of being formed. The 'newness' is not multimedia itself as there are many ways of creating illustrated stories both on and off the computer. What is important about multimedia authoring is that it creates an artefact that could not have been produced off the computer. Multimedia is particularly good at creating integrated compositions and the skills needed to do this are very useful to develop. Students will need to decide how the different media interrelate and what effect this has. They will need to consider questions such as:

• Which media will get the message across most clearly?
• Will text and sound together, for example, change the meaning from using a picture and sound?
• Which media will create the relevant mood or atmosphere?

For example, a year-5 class (9 and 10 year olds) working on adaptation drew pictures of animals in their environment. They added information in the form of pop-up text boxes so that when the user clicks on different parts of the animal a text box appears and explains how that aspect of the animal is adapted to its environment (see Screen shots 6.5 and 6.6).

Screen shots 6.5 and 6.6 Clicking on parts of the penguin reveals pop-up text boxes explaining how features adapt to climate.

If we consider this penguin, rather than a 'flat' penguin, that is simply a picture itself, the image is a 'fat' penguin as it is stuffed with knowledge waiting to be accessed giving it depth and meaning. There is a difference between a student drawing a picture of a penguin, thinking about image and colour and accuracy, as a piece of art work to stand on its own, and drawing a picture of a penguin that will hide layers of explanation. For a 'flat' image the student does not need to understand how features of penguins are adapted to their environment to draw or copy the picture, however a 'fat' image will be drawn with this knowledge so that the image itself is not the end of the story as the added words will make it into an interactive game. The actual picture outcomes may not look very different but the learning on the part of the student is.

In a 'fat' picture the image has become integrated with the text, making a word-enhanced-picture or an information-image. The penguin in this particular case only links to pop-up text boxes of explanation, but it could also link to websites on penguins making the image a gateway to the outside world. The audience, who are told to play the game, also know that the picture is not only a picture but is a puzzle with words behind it that they are trying to find and they can choose to click where they like. Although this theory may not be in the mind of a 10-year-old student drawing a penguin for a multimedia project, the multimedia penguin will take on a different significance to a non-multimedia penguin.

Just as students need to think about how to integrate text and images, they need to do the same with sound and animation. These media may be less familiar to the students, so they should consider how relevant they are and how to embed them in the piece rather than being an add-on. There are no general rules as this is context related.

Decisions may be made for aesthetic reasons or practical ones. Students who have written a lot of text may decide to read some of it because it will make the screen less cluttered. Other students may decide to have a voice-over as they think it is more likely to be understood that way. Another student may decide to have characters with bubble dialogue and sound to express what they are thinking, or a group may use sound because the audience are pre-readers.

Example 1: Annotated text and integrated composition

Project title:	*Making adventure games and stories*
Project focus:	Literacy
Age group:	Years 4–6 (8–11 year olds)
Group structure:	Small groups of four for the adventure games, pairs for the stories
Location:	Computers at the side of the classroom.
Time:	Weekly one and a half hour sessions, 6 for the adventure games, 4 for the stories

(This example is based on work by Lachs (1995) and Lachs and Wiliam (1998).)

This example describes two different projects on writing stories. In the first project groups of four students in years 5 and 6 (9–11 year olds) made multimedia adventure games that were designed to be integrated compositions. From the start the students created their own storyline by planning out a branching web structure on paper showing how the screens linked together. A typical story began with a choice of three ways to go (along the path, through the ravine or up the tree) which then led to other choices, the final aim being to find something (tigers, treasure or a drum of wisdom). Although these students had planned out the piece, they did not design the individual screens on paper, but composed them straight on to the computer. In the second project pairs of students in year 4 (8–9 year olds) wrote a linear eight-page illustrated story. They used a template where the eight screens were already linked together, with arrows at the corners to navigate forwards and backwards. Each screen (or page of the story) had a blank text box, a free space for drawing and a button to create sound. These were fixed and could not be changed. This story was text, illustrated with pictures and sound. The group did not need to plan the structure, so they simply developed the story as they went along.

Adventure stories project: integrated compositions

When presented with a blank screen and their plan, the students all began with drawing. The meaning seemed to have immediacy in the pictures, as one boy said as he was working, '*We'll draw the pictures first and then we'll know what to say*'. The stories did not initially use much text, so beginning with drawing was a natural place to start as the stories were essentially a visual medium. Drawing on the computer is not easy and took up the bulk of the 'making' time. Much of the conversation concerned how the drawing should look and which tools to use but much of it also concerned the meaning, which showed their personal involvement in the piece:

What will the cobra say?
I'm going to be the hunter.
Which bale of hay should we make the horse eat?

Minimal text accompanied the drawings, mainly in the form of instructions or directions, but as the projects progressed some students added information screens that were more textual.

The students moved between the different media easily; from creating graphics to writing text and back again, to recording sound, sequencing animation, thinking about design and back to editing their sound. An image might make students aware of the need for some text to explain it, and drawing an image showing choices of direction on the screen might not work without voice-over instructions. In these adventure stories the media did not seem to be discrete areas to be worked on separately, but rather a more complete whole as each part was adding to the meaning. This was partly achieved through the sound (generally sound effects and dialogue) being embedded in the drawings and text by way of invisible buttons. See the examples in Screen shots 6.7 and 6.8.

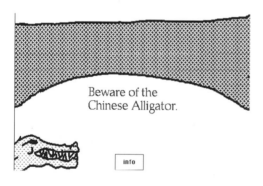

Screen shot 6.7 Minimal text, with sound on the alligator's mouth and two links – one on the 'info' button and one on the bridge.

Screen shot 6.8 Opening screen showing non-linear structure with written instructions.

One group working on the *Drum of wisdom* wanted a sound and an animation to appear together. First the group, in keeping with their original plan, drew a series of screens as an animation for a volcano erupting on the edge of an island, covering a boat and killing all the people in it. There were eight screens, each one showing the lava moving further down the mountain until it covered the boat in the sea below. Next they linked the screens together by programming the button to flick through the screens one after the other, thus completing their animation. They recorded roaring sounds and people screaming directly on to the computer and made it run at the beginning of the animation. However, after watching the animation, they decided that the sound came too early, so they switched backwards and forwards between changing the timing of the sound and watching the animation, constantly discussing where the most appropriate place for the sound was, until they got an outcome they liked. They eventually agreed that the sound should start on the third frame just as the lava began to touch the boat and needed to program this instruction into the computer. All four students in this group were engaged in the problem solving, offering suggestions and trying things out.

Story-template project: annotated text

In contrast, the pairs working on the linear story template began with writing the words to their story over the eight pages (One example is shown in Screen shot 6.9). As they had not planned the story in advance, writing out the words on each screen set the structure and essentially gave all the information that was needed. When the writing was completed the students then went back over the eight pages to add first images and then sounds. Not only was each medium worked on separately, but each medium was separate. Apart from sound, the piece was similar to making a book on the computer, however the enthusiasm it engendered in the students and the teachers was considerable. In interviewing the students, one girl, before being asked a question came in saying: '*cool. Supreme, superb*'.

Screen shot 6.9 A screen from the linear story group.

The students picked up that using sound was the main difference in this work, and they were very taken with hearing their voices on the computer. The sound was used mainly to read parts of the text aloud or to add a voice-over repetition to written dialogue. The teacher of this group also considered sound as a crucial factor: *'the idea of ownership seems to be very important, hearing themselves on tape [gives them that sense of ownership]'*.

In these two projects the adventure story groups, helped by the non-linear structure, found it easier to completely enmesh their text, sound, graphics and animation in a way that the linear story group did not. The students in the two projects also had a different sense of their part in the work. A girl in the linear project writing a story about bullying said: *'I like hearing my sound'*; showing an awareness of herself as an author. This is very different to a boy in the non-linear adventure group who identified so much with his work that, when explaining how he produced sound, said: *'I was the hunter'*. Although this response may not be connected to the difference in structure of the projects, it seems that making and integrating compositions involved these students in a very personal way.

Example 2: Design brief and choosing media

Project title:	*Genetically modified food*
Project focus:	How foods are genetically modified, the scientific and societal implications
Curriculum area:	Science
Age group:	Year 10 (14 and 15 year olds)
Group structure:	Whole class project working in pairs
Location:	Computer workshop, one computer per pair and desk space for off-computer work
Time:	Six classes over three weeks; total time 8 hours

This class had limited time and had not used multimedia authoring before, however they were confident with other computer programs and had just completed the section of science work that was the background to the project they were going to present. In the first class other students' work was viewed and discussed and each pair was given a different fruit or vegetable, some information on it and a design brief with a limited scope. The design brief gave a clear explanation of what they were to do. This was to produce four screens with text, images and sound – one title/menu screen, one screen portraying the point of view they wanted to put forward, one screen with scientific explanation and one screen with two quiz questions on the information they had written. They were told that this was the minimum, and that if they wanted to they could add more screens but only when these were completed. After this explanation they were asked to plan out their screens before they started the computer work, taking a number of factors into consideration such as how to integrate different media and to consider their audience. This design brief is reproduced in full in Appendix 1.

Although issues of design had been discussed and the students made comments and suggestions constantly as they were working together, they did not seem to have an a priori sense of what good screen design could be, instead they just used whatever came to mind. As two students explained:

> *We just try everything that we see. If it comes out good we keep it.*

> *There had to be a certain amount of variation to make our stack interesting so we just did what we thought looked good.*

Other students were very focused on designing for their audience and had a clear idea of how different media might be used for different purposes, as two other students explained:

> *Some things were better explained using pictures others words were more effective.*

> *We would think about what suited it best, like something that cannot be described by words but can by pictures and vice versa.*

These comments suggest annotated text, and indeed text was often seen by these students as the primary medium, one student said that she and her partner:

> *decided that particular information should be written because it would make it easier for people to understand and they can read at their own pace. We also did a picture so that people get it straight away what the programme is about.*

Screen shot 6.10 shows an example of a mixture of picture and text.

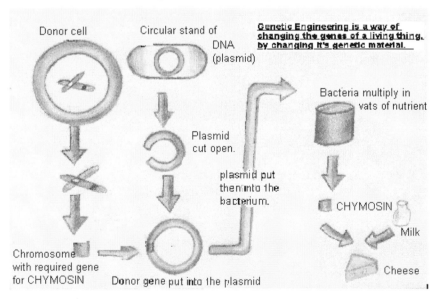

Screen shot 6.10 A picture and text mixed screen.

These students used a picture because they felt it had an immediacy that the text did not have. Text would need to be perused at the users' leisure, whereas the picture would convey the meaning right away. Another pair of students working on baked beans had scanned in a selection of real beans and used them as a background to their text. For them images held a different position:

> *We decided that particular information should be written with images to enable our readers to understand what we were saying with a better understanding and used sound to make our information more interesting.*

The idea of 'writing' with images is interesting because it implies that images are portraying the information that is usually written as text. This time, it is the sound that annotates. The same student continued using the terminology of text to describe her picture: *'You can understand a picture more. It's visual – it's easier to read'*. Their view seemed to be that images and sound all helped to create simpler 'texts'. These students' attempts to explain their work again brings up the issue of the lack of adequate language for multimedia, for example, what is that 'bit extra' this student describes? *'The writing will explain it, you find out what's going on in the picture and also a bit extra'*.

Finally, their science teacher was much more pragmatic about why the students chose particular media. He suggested that they see the potential of the program and fall for it, *'It's all there'*, he argued, *'and they want to use it all!'*

In practice . . .

1. Design brief

One of the exciting yet potentially frustrating aspects of multimedia authoring is that the plan of the whole piece and design of individual screens can constantly be added to. This can mean that it never gets finished. For example, a pair of year-5 boys working on a screen showing how traffic lights work had an image they had drawn, some explanatory text and a voice-over on their screen. They then decided to add pop-up text boxes which explained what each different colour of lights meant as the user clicked it. When this had been done, they considered animating the lights with the pop-up boxes coming in sequence. They also considered having a car driving across the screen and stopping as the lights turned red. This screen was one of six screens the pair were working on and time was, as usual, limited. At some point decisions need to be made about quantity and when to stop. This can be pre-empted by setting parameters for the students in a design brief that will limit what they can do in the project. This may include the number of screens they can use, and also specific features such as the amount of text, the use of drawing tools, and the number of animations. Encouraging students to focus on fewer tools will give them more time to consider each tool. (Appendix 1 gives an example of a design brief.)

2. Design analysis

Just as students analysed other student presentations in a consideration of audience, it is also useful to analyse work with a focus on screen design. Students in pairs should look at a presentation and agree on two screens, one they like the look of, and one they dislike and should discuss:

- What is effective in the screen they like?
- What is it that they dislike about the second screen?
- What media has the author used?
- Do the pictures and sound only illustrate or are they an integrated part of the screen?
- How could the screen design work better?
- What can they learn, both positive and negative from these screens?

3. Sketching screens

Although the plan of their piece will show the navigation routes (described in Chapter 7), it will not show the detailed content of individual screens and what media will be used. It is useful to sketch out some individual screens showing what picture, text and other features will be on that screen (see Figure 6.2). The purpose of the screen sketch is to clarify what data will need to be collected rather than to try out a design which will need to be done straight on to the computer. It is important that it is not seen as a true representation of the screen because the screen will be more integrated than the sketch will allow. This should be done with some of the screens, but not necessarily all of them.

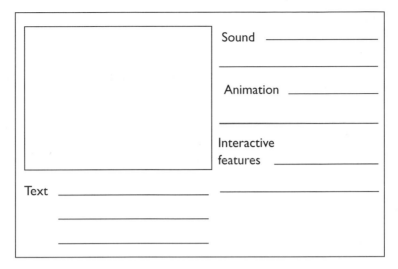

Figure 6.2 Example of a sheet for sketching a screen and clarifying what data need to be collected.

4. Elements of design

There are a number of design issues that should be taken into consideration and discussed with students. These can be explored before the work begins, however the concepts are fairly abstract and, realistically, these issues tend to be better integrated into working on creating the piece. For example, it is out of context to discuss colour or balance with students before they are part of the way through a screen and they can see for themselves how their choice of colours or where they place objects on the screen affects what the screen looks like. The practical design issues described in this chapter should be read together with other chapters on collecting data and putting the piece together as these aspects may be going on at the same time.

The final presentation should be visually appealing, easy to access and therefore easy to understand. The students need to find the most appropriate way to communicate the information and get their message across to their chosen audience. Some or all of the following issues may be relevant.

Simplicity

The screen should be easy to look at and read. People notice images before they focus in on text, and often do not read lots of text on a screen. If text is restricted to a few lines the content will need to be known very well so that it can be summarised for the important points and put into words suitable for the audience. This will encourage students not to copy from books or the Internet but to write succinctly in their own words. Short text may be simpler, but that should not detract from the character and colour of what it is trying to say as longer text can always be spread over a number of screens. The text should be typed in a clear font and style and the screen should not be cluttered with graphics. One picture over the whole screen may say more than three small images, but this decision should be made on the basis of how much the images enhance the meaning, understanding and enjoyment. In terms of the web, smaller images work better.

Balance

The 'multi' in multimedia provides variety in how to communicate ideas in the most attractive and therefore accessible way. It is sensible not to over-use any one individual form of media, making the screen feel 'unbalanced'. Students may want to use some animation and sound, but not on every screen. Thought should be given to where the information is placed on the screen. Writing can be in a text box separate from an image, or the image could take up the whole screen with the text superimposed on it, as shown in Screen shot 6.11.

Screen shot 6.11   Text superimposed on to an image.

Clarity

Information should not be duplicated unnecessarily, each medium adding rather than repeating. Less written text can be used by recording sound to give the extra details. In this way the screen will be integrated rather than annotated. If an audience of non-readers requires it, the text may be read out, as this will be an enhancement rather than a duplication. It may be that there were directions at the beginning of the program telling the user what to do and these may not be remembered later on in the piece. If necessary there should be a way to re-access these instructions.

Consistency

Generally keep the fonts, icons for buttons, colours, format and screen transitions consistent unless they are a feature of the piece. Consistent features mean that they will be less noticeable and simply used. The audience will not need to think about where to click or notice the colour of the screen. Inconsistent features produce surprise, and can be used for humour or special effect, but not too often. Consistency does not mean that the buttons are all clearly visible and the same; it does mean that the user will know what to do. An example of invisible but clearly marked buttons is shown in Screen shot 6.12.

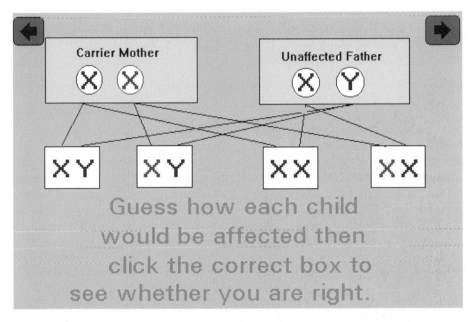

Screen shot 6.12 Invisible but clearly marked buttons.

Some features such as a flashing warning may be effective first time round, but become irritating after a while. For example, a reception class piece used a menu screen with a small self portrait by each student and the words shouted by the whole class; 'Here we are, class R'. Clicking on the portrait would go to a screen by the individual student giving further information and a larger portrait before returning to the menu screen. Each time the menu screen was accessed the sound came up. This was largely appropriate, but as the menu screen came up so often, it soon became irritating.

Meaningful navigation

Inconsistency of navigation will make the piece more difficult to use and can become frustrating. The audience needs to know what to do to move through the stack. If visible buttons are used showing where to click to move on, keep them clear but small so they do not detract from the screen itself. If the buttons are invisible, the audience will need instructions telling them what they need to do (see Screen shots 6.13 and 6.14).

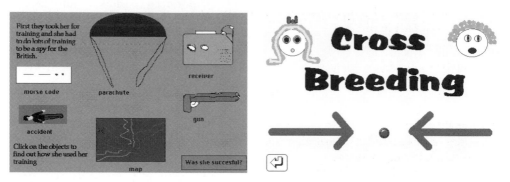

Screen shots 6.13 and 6.14 Visible and invisible buttons with clear instructions for ease of navigation.

This also applies to invisible buttons that do other things. For example, if there is an invisible sound button located over a character's mouth that gives a snippet of conversation, the user will need to be instructed to click on the mouth, otherwise they will not realise they should do so and will miss this information. Also, if there is an animation, the user needs to know what to do to see it.

Make sure that the user can exit from the program if they want to. For example, in the *Tudor maze*, there is no way out of the maze after the user has started going through it. This could become very irritating. An extra exit button is useful, however it is not always appropriate on every screen. It will be useful to have preliminary instructions on how to exit the program at any stage.

Design tips

- There needs to be discussion on issues of design and some direct teaching. A balance needs to be maintained between letting the students discover certain things for themselves and the active teaching of these concepts.
- Some colours are easier to read than others, especially when you have coloured text superimposed on a different coloured or multicoloured background. Trying the combinations out and asking others is the best way to test this as different students have different ideas on what is readable.
- Fonts can be problematic. The computer that plays the piece must have the same fonts as the one being worked on. The simplest way round this is to use basic system fonts and to keep typeface changes to a minimum.
- For a whole class project if you decide together on standard fonts and styles for buttons at the beginning, it will save a lot of time later.
- Using clipart and computer generated patterns does not infuse the piece with the students' characters. Although students love playing around with these features, they do not make for original work. However clipart can be very useful for learning skills such as importing and resizing images.

- The students need to sketch only one or two screens in advance. Once they have got the hang of it, let them try doing the design straight on screen.
- Let students become experts at particular aspects of the software so that they can help others.
- As their teacher, become analytical and critical of their on-screen work, keeping a high standard in mind.

Checklist

(Not necessarily in order):

- Design brief.
- Analyse some student work.
- Sketch out some screens.
- Discussion of integrated text and annotated composition (depending on age group).
- Consideration of design features.
- Consideration of navigation.

Chapter 7

New structures and making maps

Thinking about . . .

Western rational thought uses logic as its basis. Logic is linear, progressing from one idea to the next with causal links. We are so familiar with this way of thinking that we consider it the normal way to think, reflected in the way we write. We read books which give a narrative in sequence from page to page. A story starts at the beginning, and continues until the end whether or not the time sequence follows that order; it is expected that someone picking up a novel will not start on Chapter three, go back to Chapter two and then read Chapter five. The way the story unfolds has been crafted into the linear structure to be read in that order, letting us 'get lost' in the story, curl up with the book and be led through another world. In a similar linear fashion a written factual explanation takes the reader through ideas in sequence as they progressively build up to an understanding of greater complexity; for example, in mathematics, the concept of number needs to come before the concept of addition, and that comes before the concept of multiplication. Similarly, in using an instruction manual to put a model aeroplane together it would be nonsensical to start in the middle.

However, not all information suits a linear structure. There are times when a number of ideas could be conveyed in any order; for example, in studying the senses in secondary school science, it may not be important whether the eye is studied before or after the ear. In a different context there are times when a storyline may have a number of possible outcomes, for example some children's adventure stories in books have alternative scenarios where the reader is directed to different pages depending on their choice. In these books the reader is only led along so far and then asked to join in the story themselves by making a decision.

When we ask students to present written work we usually ask and expect them to write using a linear structure. They are taught that an essay begin with an introduction, paragraphs follow with thematic links as an argument unfolds, and it ends with a conclusion. In English, writing begins at the top of the page moving left to right and down; however, this is not always the best way to write down ideas. When working out the content for an essay, one might use a brainstorming method or make lists or cut up pieces of paper with different ideas on, before working out how to fit it all into a linear framework. Fitting ideas that are not in sequence into a linear framework can be difficult and the information may indeed need to be tweaked to make it fit. Alternative ways of presenting information that mix linear and non-linear modes would be useful in the classroom, extending the traditional linear narrative into a different type of structure. Snyder (1997) exploring the use of 'hyperfiction' in English teaching suggests that plot and story need rethinking as 'Hyperfiction apparently dispenses with linear organisation . . . Hyperfiction space is multidimensional, and theoretically infinite' (p. 28).

This new structure can be created using multimedia authoring. Students can design structures that are not wholly linear, linking smaller chunks of information by association; for example, an opening menu screen can have one broad subject area with many possible connected and relevant screens to go to at the click of the mouse. In the example on GM food quoted in Chapter 6 each pair of students worked on one theme or food. This was accessed by clicking on a tin with that word written on it (see Screen shot 7.1).

Screen shot 7.1 Menu screen for a non-linear piece where all the foods are linked by their association to the topic, which is genetic modification.

Making associations or connections between ideas, deciding what information links to what other information, has an important cognitive role. It adds an extra element to the project because it makes students consider how information is inter-related, organised and structured (Wisnudel 1994). This can make students become more engaged with the material and, in this process, the connections between concepts can become more explicit (Reader and Hammond 1994). Where information is located, and therefore linked, will be subjective and may be based on past experience, bias or personal taste and means that two people may not see the information in the same way. As these links will be made by the authors and will be used by an audience, there needs to be some consistency in how links are thought about and designed into the multimedia presentation. One student in the *Climate* project described in Chapter 3 example 1 explained how she thought about linking different screens of information:

> *You had to say, if you click here then this will come up or if you click there a button*
> *will take you to that picture . . . We had to sort out if there was a plant picture and*
> *then someone did another plant picture – you had to make that first plant picture*
> *go to the other picture so it would suit. You couldn't make a plant picture go to a*
> *weather picture or an animal one go to a clothes one.*

Although the structure for multimedia tends to be called non-linear, that only describes what it is not, rather than what it is. This can cover a wide range of possibilities, such as webs, tapestries and spirals (McGill and Weil 1989). A non-linear structure could be seen as an associative network where links are fluid. For example students may start with brainstorming ideas using spider diagrams or concept maps which then form the basis of the plan for a multimedia presentation.

It is up to the author to create association between ideas, plan them out and design them into a completed presentation, leaving the user to re-create these links by choosing a route through the piece.

The power behind authoring multimedia is that students have the opportunity to create new structures themselves, and in order to do this, they have to think creatively. It is not that students are unused to thinking in a non-linear way, but they are unused to presenting information in this way because traditional media does not readily allow them to. One teacher described her particular class:

> *They aren't academic, but very creative, they couldn't fit into boxes to get academic*
> *results, but if you let them loose, allowed them to be creative and channelled it a*
> *bit, you didn't have any resistance . . . they might not be able to explain it – but*
> *that's the way their mind works, to be honest, they're non-linear children.*

Example 1: Planning as an ongoing process

Project title: *Find the tigers*
Project focus: Making adventure games
Curriculum area: Literacy (chosen content from science)
Age group: Year 6 (age 10–11)
Group structure: A group of four students
Location: Two computers in an area outside an open-plan classroom
Time: Two hours a week for 6 weeks

(Examples 1 and 2 are based on work by Lachs (1995) and Lachs and Wiliam (1998).)

Although planning is essential at the beginning of a project, *Find the tigers* gives a good idea of how planning is a dynamic process that changes throughout a project. This particular group of students began their project in pairs at two computers exploring a multimedia story called *Cat-O-Log*, a selection of line-drawn and animated cat stories with multiple options within each showing different feline antics. They were exploring this story specifically in order to consider structure of a multimedia piece. The sound and animation in *Cat-O-Log* were activated by invisible buttons on the pictures and there was no text. The students had to guess where to click by thinking about what would happen next in the story and discussing and choosing where to click. Halfway through exploring the piece the students were shown how to press a key on the keyboard to find out where the invisible buttons were on the screen rather than having to guess. This interrupted their exploration of the story and made them focus more on considering the *structure* of the story rather than getting carried away by the content. In fact, knowing where the invisible buttons were made them more determined to explore each separate storyline as they could see how many buttons were on one screen and the potential of new storylines that lay behind these buttons. For example, on one screen there was a picture of a cat eyeing a fish in a fountain. If they clicked on the cat they got one story but if they clicked on the fish it was a completely different one. This gave rise to an amount of competition between the two pairs with *'have you found the fish getting the cat . . .'* and so on. Although the students had used multimedia programs none of them had 'decoded' them.

The students then began to plan out their own storyline together, sharing ideas, and drawing a map to show the structure of their proposed project. Their presentation was about conservation of tigers. Taking ideas from *Cat-O-Log* they wanted the user to wander around their terrain, making choices about which way to go to find tigers hidden in different places. The two girls in the group described why it was important to set up the adventure game with multiple options for the user:

> *Every time you come to a stage you have to choose where you want to go. If you were just going to one place it wouldn't be that interesting.*

> *You have to make decisions. If you've got different choices then it's better than just going one way. It makes it more funny if you've got lots of choices.*

On the opening screen of their game, they decided on three possible directions for the user to go in: along a path, up a tree or into a ravine. Along the way there would be animals other than tigers that could help them or that they would need to escape from. The students had chosen animals that they liked the sound of without doing too much research at this stage. They came up with a game structure that looked like Figure 7.1.

Having completed this first plan the group realised that the final game would be easy to play because although there were a number of options at the start, these became more limited as the user played the game. They therefore added the idea of hunters who were killing the tigers, and who the user would need to find and disarm. They looked for places on their plan where they could add extra screens close to a tiger screen to include the hunters in the story.

Only at this point did they begin making the screens, but they immediately came up with a problem. The girls began by drawing a bird but realised that they did not know what type of bird they should be drawing. The boys were drawing a snake, but again had the same difficulty. Time was then spent off the computer looking at wildlife files to determine what specific animals the generic bird or snake were and where they lived. They had assumed that the game was set in Africa, but could not find reference to a tiger. After research they chose the Bengal tiger and found that there were no crocodiles or chimpanzees but there were alligators and gibbons. They went back to their map to change it accordingly. In this process they made connections between the three separate

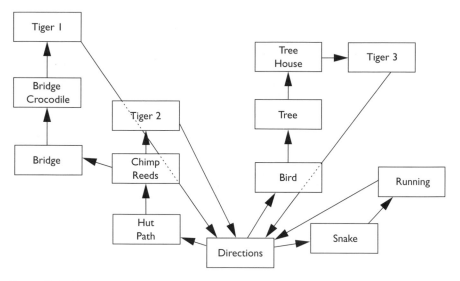

Figure 7.1   First map of *Find the tigers*.

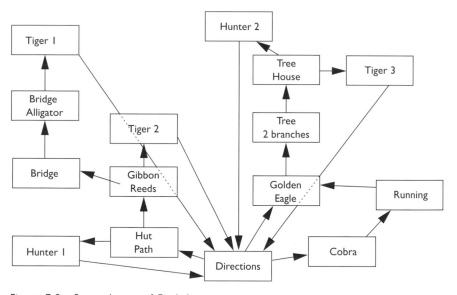

Figure 7.2   Second map of *Find the tigers*.

strands so that running away from the cobra, rather than going back to the beginning went to the tree which housed the eagle. Their map now looked like Figure 7.2.

In the process of finding pictures of the animals the students came across large amounts of information. This project was essentially a project on narrative within a literacy context, but they became interested in the subject matter and wanted to add the information they had found. As there was not enough space on the screens they had drawn, they added extra screens and extra animations. By about halfway through the project they had a much more complex map than the one they began with. This is shown in Figure 7.3 and was in fact the map of the final piece.

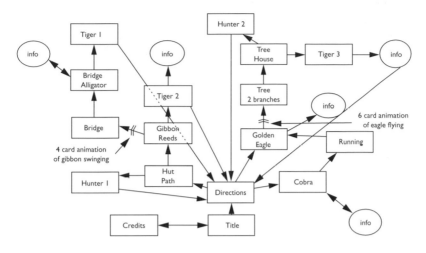

Figure 7.3 Final map of *Find the tigers.*

Although the plan changed substantially during the project, the first plan was essential because the following plans were developments on this structure, and it would have been harder to create the more complex structure without going through these different stages. The students were told at the beginning that they were limited to 12 screens. In the end the piece used 32 screens with text, images, sound and animation. The changing map helped the students to clarify the non-linear structure and keep their ideas together. They constantly referred back to it during the project to work out what screen to draw next and to see how the screens were linked. The changing and developing map clearly reflects the changing and developing ideas of the students.

Example 2: Making planning concrete for young students

Project title:	*Our playground*
Project focus:	Making a tour of the playground
Age group:	Year 2 (age 6–7)
Group structure:	A group of four students
Location:	Two computers at the side of a classroom
Time:	Two hours a week for 6 weeks

The students in this project did not go through the process of drawing maps. The teacher had decided on a topic in advance and the students were given a prototype map, shown in Figure 7.4, to explain how they were going to work.

The teacher described to the students how the boxes represented screens on the computer, and that each screen would be a different area of the playground. Their task would be to produce the pictures, text and songs to go on each screen. The students began by walking around the playground looking for and choosing their favourite areas, writing a list of these places and deciding which they would photograph and which they

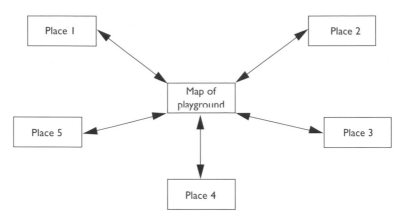

Figure 7.4 Prototype map for *Our playground*.

would draw. Before starting these pictures, however, they made the central menu screen which was a part photograph/part picture of the whole playground for them to link the individual screens back to (see Screen shot 7.2). They were excited by the concept of drawing a map of the playground and of writing about their favourite places, but initially they had difficulty conceptualising how the whole piece would look.

Screen shot 7.2 Opening screen of *Our playground*.

With help they slowly built up a plan, developing the prototype which ended as Figure 7.5.

This project was strongly linked to tangible places that the students knew well. This made it concrete and real in the students' minds by making the work on the computer and the work off the computer connected. They could say, 'well I can walk to this part

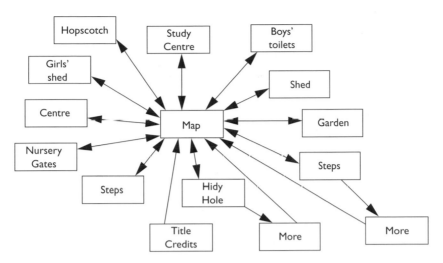

Figure 7.5 Final map for *Our playground.*

of the playground and then I can come back', and they could see the arrows on their plan taking them there and back. By the end they had got a sense of how the structure worked, as they explained:

> *We done a map. When you click it . . . when you press on any picture then it will take you there.*

> *It was good going to the other side of another page. Any button you pressed would go on to another page.*

In practice . . .

Although linking screens together in a non-linear format offers a succinct new way of presenting branching stories, multiple perspectives, opposing ideas or different aspects of the same theme, there is a potential pitfall. Associative networks open infinite possibilities for design, infinite routes through material and infinite ways of getting lost. Without an adequate plan students can forget what links to what, what screens they have completed and what they have left to do, so it is important to start simple and plan carefully. A map of hyperspace will become an essential help and aide-memoire in the process of construction.

Maps have different purposes. An A–Z map of London shows a different view to a tube map. Both are fit for purpose but their purposes are different. The maps, storyboards and plans that students need to design will depend on their function. They might show:

- the structure of routes between screens of information
- interactive elements
- animation sequences
- sketches of the basic content on each screen.

This plan will also change as the piece develops. It is sensible to start small and let things be added if necessary.

1. Analysis of structure

A useful start is to look at student work again, specifically thinking about structure; that is the route the piece takes, how it moves from screen to screen. Take a simple student project and demonstrate with the whole class, mapping out the movement between screens and drawing the plan out on a flipchart or chalkboard so that they can take in the process of analysis. They should understand the shorthand you are using. I use a rectangle to denote a screen with a few key words to say what is on that screen, an arrow to show a link to another screen, and multiple arrows to show the use of animation as a link to another screen. Pairs of students should then draw out maps of a simple multimedia presentation, again showing only the screens and the links. It is important that the piece chosen for analysis is small and manageable. There are example pieces to use on the CD ROM enclosed with this book. The maps for these pieces are drawn out in Appendix 2.

The object of this exercise is not for the students to 'get it right', it is for them to start thinking about structure. By part way through this exercise they may get involved with the content of the piece they are analysing and forget to draw screens, they may see lots of things they think they can do better and will get ideas that they want to copy. But this is not yet the time for them to leap into designing their own maps because it is important to realise that they have just analysed the *final version* of another group's work, and there are some preliminary stages they need to go through.

2. Brainstorming

The first task is to specify the broad content areas of the subject for the multimedia presentation. This can be done by brainstorming with the students. It is useful to do this with the whole class in order to give each student the overall idea so that when they are producing their small part, they can have a sense of where that will fit in. Traditionally brainstorming takes the shape of a spider graph with a central word, and many words around the outside coming from it. Any contribution that is connected to the subject should be encouraged at this stage. The outcome will be something that looks like a complicated jumble, as shown in Figure 7.6.

Brainstorming has started the students thinking, but they are as yet unstructured, unconnected thoughts which need to be tightened into a workable plan. The next stage is to look for links between these ideas and group them accordingly, creating something that begins to look more like a concept map such as Figure 7.7.

Although this is starting to look like a multimedia plan, it is only an initial brainstorm of ideas that has begun to define distinct themes. It is not yet split into the information that will be produced on individual screens.

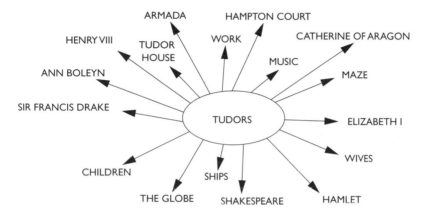

Figure 7.6 Tudor brainstorm.

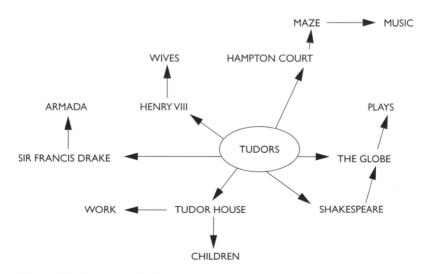

Figure 7.7 Grouping the brainstorm.

3. Drawing maps for multimedia

There are many possibilities for planning out a multimedia project. The important feature is to design the structure off the computer so that the paper can be passed round the group, pinned up on the wall, clearly visible so that everyone in the group or class has an idea of the overall look of the piece even if they will not be working on all of it. Examples of students' plans are given in Appendix 3, and Plate 7.1 shows a student at work.

Plate 7.1 A student drawing out a multimedia plan.

For any project, third timers as well as first timers, it is sensible to start with a limited number of screens. Keep the project small and manageable. It will grow if it seems possible to add more, and will stay small and succinct if that is what works for that particular group or class. It is definitely easier to add than to pull back from a plan that is too extensive. First timers may choose a simple linear three or four screen presentation. Older students can also start small, using a similar number of screens but making them non-linear with a menu screen and three links. This process is similar whether working with whole classes, small groups, pairs or even individuals. There are a number of possible structures.

Linear with branches

This structure is the most basic beyond a totally linear piece – essentially a straightforward linear storyline with added extras (see Figure 7.8). This is useful for young students working on stories and extending the narrative by adding alternate endings. It may be a good way in for first timers who want to keep a simple structure so that the concentration can be on other aspects of multimedia authoring before moving on to more complex structures.

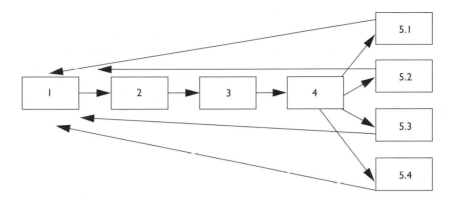

Figure 7.8 Linear map with branches.

This form of plan can use the linear structure to hold the main theme and have small linear offshoots with extra themes. This suits group work well as it can be easily split into parts. For example, a year-3 class working on the Armada told the story of a boy on a Tudor ship in six screens. Other information was produced on screens that were linked to each story screen. This class was split into 7 groups, one worked on the storyline and one group on each of the other themes (Figure 7.9).

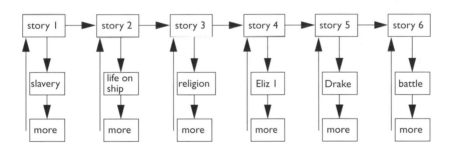

Figure 7.9 Armada example of linear map with branches.

The *Tudor maze* project described in the introduction was essentially linear with offshoots, however the user may not have been aware of this as there were at least two, usually three, possible directions on each screen (see Figure 7.10).

Although there were many options, this was still essentially a linear structure with offshoots as can be seen clearly from the student-drawn map of the maze to help users know where they are (Screen shot 7.3).

Hierarchical

A hierarchical structure splits information into smaller linear chunks using menu screens as a way of listing information that will follow. A prototype would look something like the map in Figure 7.11.

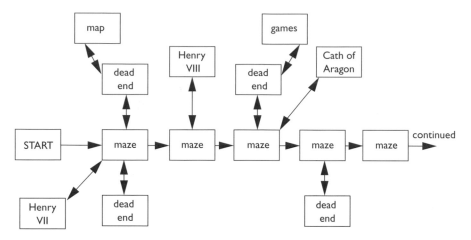

Figure 7.10 Maze example of linear map with branches.

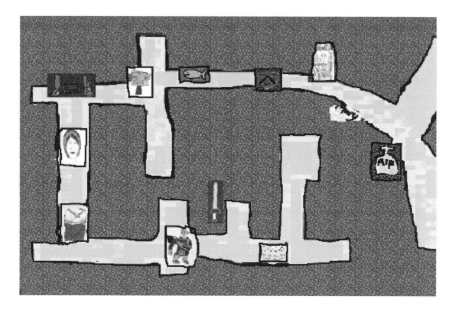

Screen shot 7.3 Student-drawn map of Tudor maze that can be accessed at various points in the piece.

This structure defines the overall category, splitting into sub-categories and sub-sub-categories, and so on. Notice that the arrows are two way, allowing the user to move both backwards and forwards. The plan could also allow the user to go from the sub-sub-categories back to the main subject. It does not offer linking across themes. This structure can be useful for group work as it clearly defines discrete areas. For example, a year-6 class used the River Thames as their central menu screen, which linked off to buildings on the Thames, linking in turn to more specific information about those buildings (see Figure 7.12)

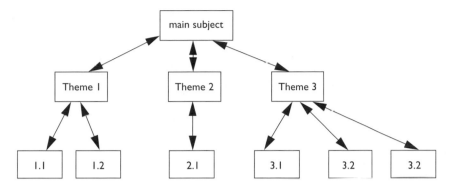

Figure 7.11 Hierarchical map.

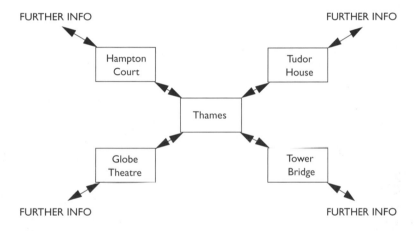

Figure 7.12 Hierarchical map of Tudor London.

Web structure

A web structure is the most free flowing and flexible and offers the most choice in direction. It is the structure of large masses of information such as encyclopaedias and the World Wide Web. It is also the most difficult to keep control of as screens are linked to others in no consistent way. *Find the tigers* is an example of this type of structure as there are links between each strand of storyline. Web structures are not simple to make, and not simple to navigate, and may be difficult to use for classroom projects. An important rule of thumb is that functionality is central, and that there should not be extraneous and unnecessary links. A small web structure is shown in Figure 7.13.

Although the different structures have been described separately, many multimedia presentations will have a mixed structure, with some parts hierarchical but, within that, will be linear or web-type features.

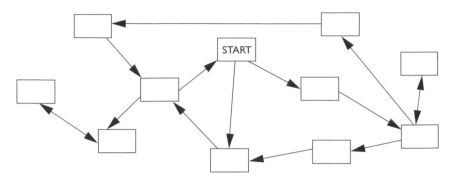

Figure 7.13 Web structure.

Alternative planning

In all of these diagrammatic maps screens are shown by rectangular boxes linked by arrows, but there are alternative ways of notating plans. Younger students can use cardboard to cut out boxes and link them together with string to make the structure more concrete and explicit. The *Climate* project had sets of plans, the first being boxes linked by arrows. The second set comprised of artwork that had been scanned into the computer, then stuck on to large sheets of paper, with links drawn in between the pictures, as shown in Plate 7.2.

Plate 7.2 Artwork stuck on to a planning sheet.

However it is done, the plan will be valued and referred to often. Sharing the plan with a group is easier on a tangible paper document that can be passed around and put up on the wall.

Planning tips

- Start small and simple.
- Limit the number of screens students can use; start with one for each group member.
- It is easier to begin with a branching story than a web structure.
- Let the plans expand organically during the project if the students are producing quality work. If not, they should re-do screens rather than making additions to their plans.
- If plans change, it should be on account of their purpose and function, not just because the students want to make the piece larger.

Checklist for the planning stage

- Analyse other students' work and sketch out the plan of it on paper.
- Brainstorm the topic for this project.
- Group it into different areas.
- Split the class into groups of these areas for a whole class project.
- In these groups, work out more detailed plans.
- Share ideas with whole group, getting constructive feedback.
- Change plans if necessary.

Chapter 8

Interactivity

Thinking about . . .

School students will be used to having some degree of physical control over technology, whether it is changing channels or adjusting the volume on the television, programming a video recorder or playing a computer game. Students will be used to interactive computer games, in fact, their hand–eye co-ordination may have been perfected some years ago by jumping strange creatures over weird terrains while dodging aliens. Computer games are the culture with which they are familiar, and they will be completely expert in some of the games and bored with others. In this arena students usually know more than their teachers, but rather than seeing this as a problem, it can be used to good advantage. The curriculum computer software created with multimedia authoring will be a very different sort of animal from the repetitive jumping and fighting games, but students seem to bring the computer confidence and motivation gained from these games with them into the multimedia authoring project in the classroom.

The difference between interactive multimedia and linear narrative is that the interactive multimedia 'does not exist meaningfully without the interactions of the learner' (Plowman 1996, p. 95). In other words, the game cannot be played without a player. The term 'interactive' used in relation to computer programs or games is generally thought to mean what the user needs to physically do in order to use the program or play the game, sometimes described as 'user control'. This physical inter-activity may include clicking on navigation buttons, clicking on objects to make things happen, dragging objects around the screen or writing answers to questions. However this is simply the surface for a deeper level of interactivity, that is mental interaction with the material: grappling with ideas, making decisions, choosing directions and considering options. These activities can be additionally facilitated by interacting with another person, discussing the ideas and collaborating on joint decisions.

For example, at one computer a student can use a program where he or she has to read text from the screen, think about the content and respond to it, making a decision by clicking on the appropriate way forward. This may be a question in a quiz, a choice of direction in an adventure story or setting up a variable in a modelling program. There may be a right or wrong answer, there may be no correct answer, or it may be testing a hypothesis. All these possibilities involve the user in thought, choice and action. The computer is creating some of the interaction (drag the weather symbols on to the map of Brazil), and encouraging or mediating other interaction (find out about what the weather is like in summer in Brazil). Of course, not all interactivity (such as repetitive computer games) makes you think!

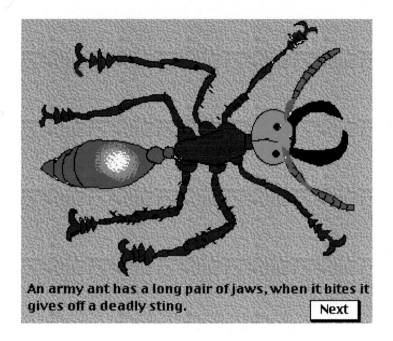

An army ant has a long pair of jaws, when it bites it gives off a deadly sting.

Next

Screen shots C1 and C2 Images drawn straight on to the computer using the mouse vary in sophistication, but are full of character

King Richard the 2nd and the lead up to the peasants revolt.

Next

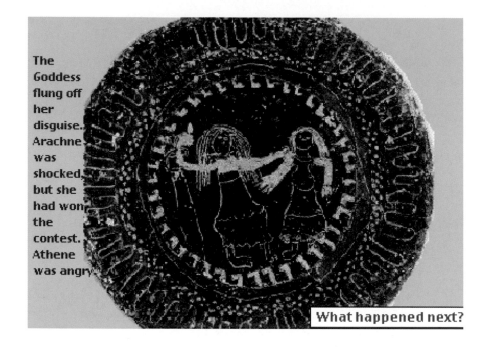

Screen shots C3 and C4 Artwork produced off the computer and scanned in can use many different media: examples here are wax etching and felt collage

This is a cooking pot on the fireplace. These things are over 400 years old. Sarah is wearing the clothes of a rich boy in the tudor times.

To maze

Screen shots C5 and C6 Using photographs taken with a digital camera to make photo montages. The tudor picture combined two photographs of the kitchen and one of a pot

Back

1 2 3

BACK FROM THE DEAD
An interview with Tutankhamun

Click on heads to hear the interview.

4

To get into the tomb you need
a password.
Choose the right hieroglyphs
which will give you the
Answer.
What are some people buried
in after death?

Help with heirogliphics

WARNING! WARNING!
If you get the password wrong the sphinx
will chase you back to the beginning.

Screen shot C7 Text for different purposes, showing clues (blue box), advice (red box) and instructions (green button)

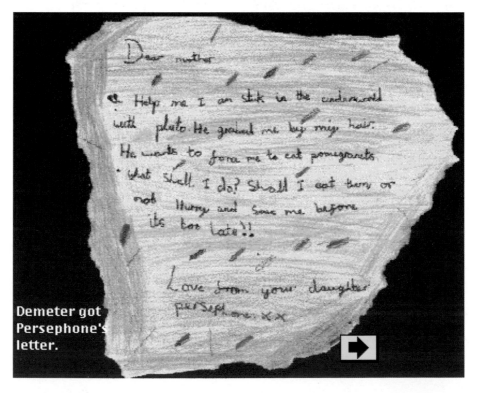

Demeter got
Persephone's
letter.

Screen shot C8 Handwritten letter scanned on to the computer

Despite students' familiarity with computer games or CD ROMs or the Internet, they are not, as a general rule, familiar with making software. When students are making computer programs for someone else there is an additional layer to what they need to do. Not only is there the students' active engagement with the program they are using – planning, designing screens, discussing content and considering links – they are also having to consider how their eventual audience will interact with the piece when they use it, both mentally (what will they think about?) and physically (what will they do?). They therefore need to consider how to engage their audience in the process that they themselves are going through. Although students have a tacit knowledge of interactive elements of computer games they may never have thought about it explicitly. The process of bringing this out in discussion, making the workings of computer programs more obvious and transparent, is an essential element in students' ability to generate thoughtful and creative software which will make an engaging product for their audience as well as involving themselves in the process.

It frequently happens that the sort of on-screen interactivity students are familiar with in computer games is much more complex than student multimedia or web authoring programs can offer. Although students may not be able to reproduce exactly what they see in professional programs, there is an opportunity for creative problem solving, finding ways round their initial idea to make something that works well enough, or changing their idea so that it fits into the framework they are working with.

Squires (1996) argues that the level of control that students have in their interaction with software when they are *using* a multimedia or hypertext program will help them feel that they are 'instrumental in determining the pattern and progress of the learning experience' which will give students the 'confidence and awareness to reflect on the learning process' (p. 13). As he is talking here about *using* multimedia, how much more appropriate is this statement if we consider students *making* the interactive multimedia themselves.

Examples: Creating interactivity

In the planning stage of a number of projects students were asked to focus on creating a game out of historical, geographic or scientific material, where the player would be active and engaged so that their interest would be sustained. To make the ideas of interactivity explicit most classes discussed computer games and the interactive elements they were familiar with before analysing interactive elements in other student projects. Despite the simplicity of the interactivity in other students' work, some students came back with fairly complex ideas. One group working on the Sun made up a story where a curse had been put on the Earth by an alien and voyagers were sent into space to try to find a way to reverse the curse and save the Earth. They had to visit the Sun, find information, pick up extra-terrestrial objects, escape the aliens and get back to Earth before them.

These ideas had come from stories, films or more complex computer games and although they would be impossible to reproduce with simple multimedia authoring programs, they were a good start in getting the students thinking along the lines of interactivity. The students were describing what they wanted as if they were telling the story of a computer game from a user's perspective rather than thinking about being an author and what would go on individual screens. The ideas were forced into a more manageable format when they planned out individual screens on paper with arrows to link them together. The curse on the Earth became an initial storyline in text and pictures to introduce the user to information gathering about gravity and space. The escape from the aliens disappeared. The process of modifying initial ideas that were unworkable proved to be a useful way for the students to explore the software and learn what they could and could not do with it, focusing their ideas and creativity on to what they could do.

Curriculum area:	Geography
Project:	Climate
Age:	Year 5 (9 and 10 year olds)
Group structure:	Whole class working in small groups
Location:	Small computer room and classroom

Towards the beginning of the *Climate* project the students were shown how to make an image dragable so that the user would be able to move it around the screen. Every group wanted to make dragable objects. One group decided that they wanted the user to be able to clothe a person in the correct clothing for the climate by dragging articles of clothing over to a figure. They drew a mixture of clothes for different types of weather and made it all dragable. Their initial idea was that they wanted the clothing to fly back to its original place if it was for the wrong type of weather and stay on the figure if it was correct. This proved to be too difficult to do without knowing the software's internal programming language, which was beyond the scope, ability and time available for this class. The group had to come up with an alternative idea that let the user clothe the person by dragging any of the clothes on to the figure, whether they were right or wrong (see Screen shot 8.1).

Screen shot 8.1 Game to drag clothes on to the person.

This was a familiar theme, students having to adapt their ideas to make them workable, as a boy in a different group said:

> I had an idea for a game. It was hard. The original idea was that we made it so hard you'd go all the way back to the beginning and it'd all shuffle and start again. But we didn't know how to make that, so we made it more simple by staying on the same screen and doing it all from there. We tried something and it didn't work out so we did it simpler.

This student seemed content with the simpler game, and as a general rule students took the interactivity as a challenge rather than being too committed to any one idea.

Curriculum area:	History
Project:	*Ancient Egypt*
Age:	Years 5 and 6 (9–11 year olds)
Group structure:	Whole class working in small groups
Location:	Two-computer classroom

In this project five groups each worked on a five-screen structure where every member of the class made one screen. The format was a menu screen with four linked screens. About halfway through the project when this simple structure was completed, their teacher asked the students to go back to the planning stage and think of adding an extra game element. As the students were already used to using the software they came out with more workable ideas straight away.

The pyramids group had a menu screen with four options, as shown in Screen shot 8.2:

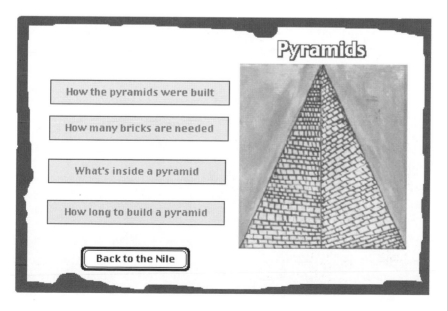

Screen shot 8.2 Menu screen for the pyramids group of the Egypt program.

Each of these options was one screen only, so the structure was very simple (see Figure 8.1)

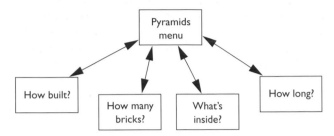

Figure 8.1 Plan of the pyramids group.

In adding an interactive game element they decided that the user would not be able to get into the pyramid without finding a password, and the password would be written in hieroglyphics. There was another group in the class working on hieroglyphics, so the two groups worked together to organise the game. This involved adding two extra screens and a link to one of the screens from the hieroglyphics group. Now, when the button was clicked on to look inside the pyramid, you were brought to a sphynx guarding it who demanded a password. However as the students would need help with the hieroglyphics, the password screen linked to a hieroglyphics alphabet so that the user could go backwards and forwards between the screens to decipher the code. If the correct password was chosen, it moved to the next screen, if not, the user was sent back to the beginning of the program. The structure now looked like Figure 8.2.

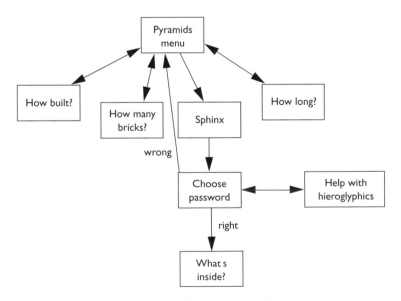

Figure 8.2 Final game structure for the pyramids group.

The important thing about this redesigned structure was that rather than the structure changing because the students wanted to make the project bigger, or had found out more information or wanted to change the links in some screens, the new structure was specifically about giving the user more to do (choosing a password) and more to think about (deciphering hieroglyphics); that is, creating greater interactivity.

These students did not find this as difficult to do as the climate groups had said they did. This was largely because the group had already mastered the concept of screens linking together with buttons before they went back to their plans to add extra interactivity. Their teacher describes the importance of prior knowledge of the software: *'It was the buttons that were crucial. Once they got the idea of the buttons it gave them another dimension. They could see how to make the buttons work for them'*.

Curriculum area:	Geography
Project:	Rainforests
Age:	Year 6 (10 and 11 year olds)
Group structure:	Whole class working in small groups
Location:	One-computer classroom

This class wanted to produce a quiz structure where the students were given some information, asked a question about it, and if they got it right, were rewarded with an animation. For example, one student working on a bee made an animation of the bee flying to a flower with a voice-over explaining about collecting pollen. This was followed by a written question on the screen about where honey comes from. There were three possible answers. If the wrong one was clicked on there was a voice-over explanation as to why it was wrong. If the right answer was chosen the user was given another explanatory animation followed by another question.

In a similar vein two other students were working on the life cycle of a butterfly. The first student made an animation of the process, but rather than having a straightforward question, the second student was making a drag and drop game where the user had to put the life cycle in the correct order. The only problem with the game was that they did not know what to do when the user got it wrong, as the programming to make the game really work was much too complex. This did not stop the students being very pleased with their game as it stood and they tried it themselves over and over again and showed it to other members of their class (see Screen shot 8.3).

These examples have specifically shown the physical interactivity the students created, but the interactivity between them and the material during this process was very evident. To illustrate this, here is a small extract of conversation between two students working on a food chain. The first student was explaining to the second what she had done.

Student 1: *This is the food chain, the spider eats the bird.*
Student 2: *The spider eats the bird? No the bird eats the spider.*
Student 1: *It's a bird-eating spider. There's also a snake and a fly. The bird eats the fly, the spider eats the bird, the snake eats the spider and then what will we do with the snake?*
Student 2: *That's the end of the food chain. They [younger students] will have to put them in order.*
Student 1: *Then press enter and then . . . they'll get it right or wrong.*

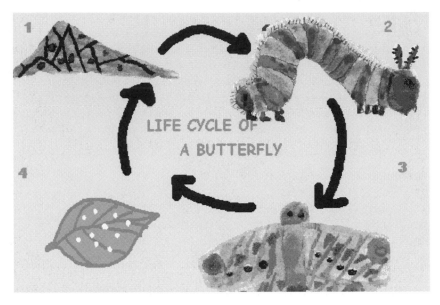

Screen shot 8.3 Drag and drop game to put the life cycle in the right order.

In this example, the creation of the game and the need to explain it to each other seemed to facilitate the students to discuss the content.

Curriculum area:	ICT
Project:	*Using multimedia authoring/Cell division*
Age:	Year 12 (17 year olds)
Group structure:	Small class working in pairs
Location:	Computer room

As part of his ICT project a student wanted text boxes that popped up with 'Yes' and 'No' when you clicked on the possible answers. He realised, however, that when he moved to another screen and then returned to his first screen, the Yes or No had stayed there. It was possible to program the software so that the words would disappear when the user left the screen but as he did not know how to do that, he thought up the more creative solution of animating the words (see Screen shot 8.4). This was in fact a more complex way round the problem but a way that he could manage on his own.

These examples describing students creating on-screen interactivity for their audience show how much problem solving becomes part of a multimedia authoring project. The students were motivated to find solutions, not because they were given a problem to solve, but because they had created the problem for themselves, and it was the limitations of the software that encouraged them to find ways round their initial ideas. These examples of interactivity (and more) are on the CD ROM.

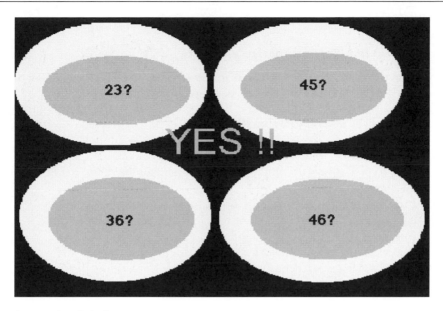

Screen shot 8.4 Quiz screen on a project on mitosis.

In practice . . .

1. Brainstorm familiar interactive elements

The question to ask is, what interactive features are there in computer games? Students are likely to give some or all (and more) of the following answers:

- you can go in at different levels
- if you get something wrong, you get sent back to the beginning
- you have to choose which way to go
- you have to pick things up on the way, and when you have too many you have to decide which item to drop
- you can choose a character you are going to be
- you cannot go on until you have got the right answer in a quiz
- you can move your character around
- you can explore a room by clicking on things
- you can play with a partner
- you need to find out the password
- you can make a new character.

Encourage all answers because, as shown in the examples, although some of these features are not possible on simple multimedia or web authoring packages, the students' imagination is often ahead of their ability to deliver, and the ideas they come up with will be helpful in focusing on seeing themselves as the creators rather than the audience. This will also encourage students to be flexible with their ideas and solve the problems creatively.

2. Stack analysis

The next step in making the interactivity explicit is to look at some CD ROMs or websites authored both by professionals and by students of a similar age group to analyse what interactivity is being used. The students need to critically deconstruct work by others, looking at both positive and negative features of the interactivity. When students begin to look at a piece of software they often get involved in the action of it, so they may need to be reminded that they are answering specific questions and trying to leave to one side whether or not they are interested in the subject.

Criteria for analysing software looking at interactivity

- What did you have to do as a player?
- What did you have to think about?
- Did you know what to do? Where to click?
- Were the navigation buttons clearly marked?
- Did you have enough to do or too much?
- Were the interactive elements connected to the subject?
- Were the interactive elements fun?
- Could it have worked without those interactive elements?
- What would you have added or taken away in terms of interactivity?

3. Consider interactivity for their own pieces

Although it is useful if the brainstorm and analysis of interactivity happen early on in the project, for first timers you may want to delay this stage until they are a little more familiar with the software as this will be the limiting factor on what on-screen interactivity they can produce. Alternatively, this may be a stage that is repeated twice, first in order to get general ideas, and later to be more practical and to work out how to tweak those first ideas into a something that can be achieved. The answers to the questions obtained from analysing other multimedia pieces or websites will inform their own pieces and give them ideas. They will need to be clear about what they want the audience to think about so that they produce interactive features in order to facilitate understanding, and clarify and encourage participation rather than making interactivity for interactivity's sake.

Interactivity tips

- When discussing concepts, make sure that the key points are brought out by moving the discussion on if necessary.
- Giving students an opportunity to understand interactivity in its wider sense may help with their own engagement with the material and groupwork.
- Interactive features can be very simple, just moving between screens and having options of which way to go is enough. This alone can become complex.
- Although students might like to make dragable items, when everything is dragable it gets repetitive. Students often get hooked on a special effect and use it because they enjoy making it. They should be reminded that interactivity is directly related to the audience for the piece, that design is important and that their audience will not want to drag everything!
- You may want to limit the students to one 'games' feature per group.

Checklist

- Brainstorm possible interactive features in computer games.
- Discuss what interactivity is, widening the concept of physical interactivity with the screen to include interactivity with the ideas and the material.
- Analyse a familiar game or work by other students.
- Consider the sort of interactivity wanted in their own pieces.

Chapter 9

Collecting information and creating the presentation

Thinking about . . .

In order to collect information, students need to know what they want to collect. This can take a circuitous route as gathering some information can lead to other information, open new avenues or make students reflect differently on what they have already found out. At the point of information collection and transfer on to the computer, everything can change. O'Neill (1998) describes the scenario of students using a digital camera, importing the images on to the computer and then having to decide what to do with the images. He claims, no doubt from experience: 'Typically the discussion surrounding the editing of such images is very animated' (p. 146). Indeed it may happen that as the image is being edited on the screen, and the students can see the effect it makes, they

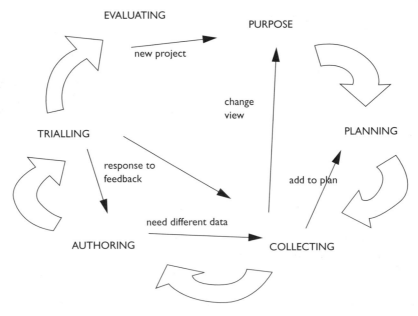

Figure 9.1 Processes involved in creating a project. The main direction of the project is offset against the back and forth movement of changing and developing ideas.

realise that the image they really want is something different, so discard that one and take another picture. There is no simple flowchart that leads from purpose to planning, collecting information, authoring, trialling and evaluating, as there is too much to and fro for this to be straightforward. The process looks more like the non-linear jumble in Figure 9.1. The circle of large arrows shows the general direction of a multimedia authoring project. The thin arrows show the process of problem solving and modification of ideas. This becomes a dynamic non-linear flow which is typical of the process of creativity and learning.

Although a multimedia project is best as an integrated composition, each medium will need to be created separately and used for what it can do best. Images, sound, text, animation and video all speak to the viewer in different ways and it is this difference that adds to the richness of the piece and infuses it with the personalities of the authors. For example, images can be broad where text can add detail, or the sound can give background explanation where images show the specific detail. In a project on electricity two boys chose to draw a kitchen where clicking on each appliance changed the image to the workings of the appliance with text explaining how that appliance used electricity. In this case the text gave the details the picture could not (see Screen shots 9.1 and 9.2).

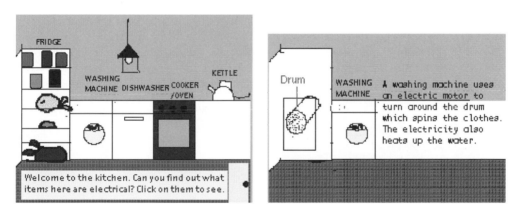

Screen shots 9.1 and 9.2 Electricity – text explaining details.

In the same multimedia presentation two girls chose to animate an electric circuit. This shows what happens when the switch is pressed. An explanation comes up as sound, and text is only needed to give directions on where to click (see Screen shots 9.3 and 9.4).

Heppell (1994) offers a different perspective, claiming that multimedia is not at all new, and although no one describes 'life as a multimedia experience', it no doubt is. He argues that rather than consider how each medium can contribute to the whole, we might ask 'in what circumstances might it be appropriate to leave something out?' This is an interesting perspective because if the norm is all-media, then leaving something out will need to be justified. Being realistic, schools and the curriculum may not be able to accommodate total inclusiveness, and the justification for leaving out video may simply be that there is not enough time.

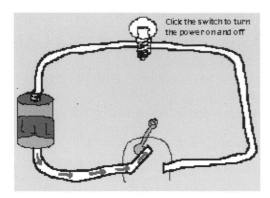 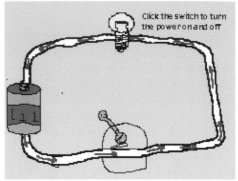

Screen shots 9.3 and 9.4 Electricity – images explaining concept.

Images

Images are powerful, they reflect what the author wants to say and they convey impressions without needing to be explicit. Images can have more than one meaning and are more open to interpretation than precise text. As discussed in Chapter 6, the images should be integrated with other media and this must be kept in mind. Pictures are almost always the first features that the audience will notice as they move from screen to screen and this gives them an important role in terms of communication. Students often draw pictures of themselves, and this adds to their feeling that the work is theirs, has some meaning in their lives and makes them visible (see Screen shots 9.5 and 9.6). Generally images can:

- provide a background
- illustrate an idea
- introduce characters
- tell a story
- show details
- give clues
- create atmosphere.

 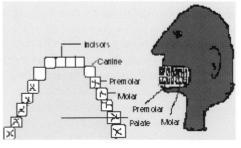

Screen shots 9.5 and 9.6 Students putting themselves in the picture.

Animation

Making an animation is a way of *showing* what is happening rather than describing it. Unlike video which shows actual events, animation is particularly useful for showing processes and dynamic concepts that:

• are too slow to see, such as a plant growing or continents moving apart over millions of years
• are hidden, such as the digestive system or the inside of a piece of machinery
• happened a long time ago, such as the big bang
• are too fast to see, such as an insect flapping its wings
• are too small to see, such as the movement of electrons in an atom
• cannot be explained in one dimension, such as rotating an image
• need to be represented, such as time passing by a clock's hands moving round.

Making these animations is a good way for students to clarify their understanding because they will need to know each step of the process to be able to put it in order and this may also be helpful for the teacher as part of assessment (see Screen shot 9.7).

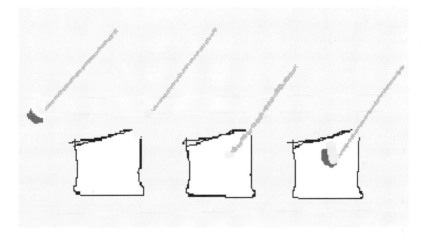

Screen shot 9.7 Animation in four screens of re-lighting a glowing splint.

Animation does not only show processes. Children are familiar with cartoons that tell stories and the animation adds character and humour. A science class looking at adaptation considered animals in their environment before seeing what would happen if that animal was put into an alien environment. They used animation to show the result of a fish in the air parachuting to the ground and a seal in the desert getting sunburnt. Needless to say, this can be fun and motivating for the students.

Text

If a picture says a thousand words students may not need to use that much text. The limitations of both people's attention-span for reading text on the screen and available space can be used to good advantage. If students know that they must explain a concept in five lines, they will need to be concise and work out what the essential information is, as well as keeping the piece entertaining and keeping their audience in mind. Text can be written in whatever style students want, as a story, a report, a review, a letter or an interview transcript, to name a few. The ideas may be complex, but the way they are transmitted needs to be accessible. Text covers many functions:

- titles for the whole piece or individual screens
- instructions ('Click the ladybird', 'Use Mr keys to turn on the car engine and drive to the bank')
- explanations ('Oxygenated blood carries a lot of oxygen and very little carbon dioxide')
- reports of events ('Rosa's refusal to give up her seat helped start a movement against segregation')
- questions ('Where do you want to go next?' 'Where does honey come from?')
- dialogue (bubbles coming from characters' mouths)
- storyline ('It was Monday morning and Nadege and Matthew were playing hopscotch while waiting for the bell to ring')
- labels (labelled diagram of the earth's layers)
- advice ('you may want to check . . .')
- warnings ('Beware of the hunters')
- reminders ('Did you find all five shapes in this story?')
- clues ('The password is what the ancient Egyptians were buried in after they died').

Sound

Sound as words can serve similar functions to written text, however there are two crucial differences. First, although an explanation can be read, *hearing* the same explanation can be easier to understand and more memorable. The way a person speaks is not identical to how they write, they may use more colloquial words when speaking and this can have a more personal effect. Second, when students speak on the computer they place themselves in their piece in a more obvious way as the audience will be able to hear (and maybe recognise) their voices. Students enjoy putting sound into their presentations, possibly due to the novelty of multimedia authoring. Sound can confer status to dialect, language and that individual person, and this brings with it a sense of ownership and pride. Adding the spoken word to multimedia pieces adds character, interest and entertainment and can be used in a number of ways.

- Voice-over explanations or instructions can clearly show how much a student understands by hearing how they explain it.
- Role plays of characters in a story give students the chance to act out their storyline.
- Interviews give a sense of the person and the way they speak and can include hearing the person's first language.
- Translation. Text can be read in other languages to make it accessible to a wider range of people. If the piece is written in Urdu, the sound can be a translation into English for non-Urdu speakers. If the piece is written in English, there could be a number of different language options spoken as alternatives to the text.
- Reading the text for non-readers.

- Warnings, instructions or reminders written on the screen may be reinforced by a person's voice.
- Singing a title song, jingo or rap.

Non-voice sounds can add atmosphere and help in navigation, such as:

- background music
- sound effects
- functional sounds, such as a button click as screens change.

It must be kept in mind that, although the sound should be integrated, if the project is too reliant on sound, it will be inaccessible to students with hearing impairment, as well as being hard to hear in a busy classroom.

Video

Video is the most powerful way of students putting themselves in the picture, as they can be actors in their own drama. They can show familiar locations with a panoramic view and give status to these characters and locations. Video is already an integrated medium, thought must go into integrating the video into the multimedia setting.

Example 1: Animation to clarify science

Project title: *The Moon*
Project focus: The Moon in space
Curriculum area: Science
Age group: Year 5 (9 and 10 year olds)
Group structure: A group of four students
Location: At side of classroom on two computers
Time: One morning a week for 7 weeks

(This piece came runner-up in the European Multimedia Awards 1997. The example is based on Lachs (1999).)

This project was a taster to the subject of space that would be the science curriculum work for the following half term. Four mixed ability students were to make a multimedia presentation for the class to use as an introduction to the subject. This meant that the students were researching the material throughout the production process. They only used books as the computers did not have CD ROM drives, nor were they connected to the Internet. The students read the text, and put it into their own words or pictures to explain it. The students drew straight on to the computer with the mouse, animated key concepts such as eclipses and orbits, wrote explanations of these concepts and added voice-over commentaries. The class teacher maintained that: '*It gave them an incentive to do more research than normally on a topic*'.

Drawing with a mouse is a challenge. The students get used to it and enjoy it but do not find it easy, as they explain:

Student 1:   *The drawings were hard, especially the lava one and it was hard to make that fat scribble.*

Student 2:   Yeah, it was grey deep within the rock and orange on the surface.
Student 1:   And you had to put it spilling over the grey bit.
Student 3:   It wasn't like a proper pencil, the mouse is hard to draw with.

One scene from their project is shown in Screen shot 9.8.

The moon has no air or living things and it also has no water. The dark areas of the Moon are vast dry plains. Early astronomers thought they were seas and oceans. The seas and oceans were formed as a result of giant meteorite impacts. The biggest of these were so violent that they cracked the Moon's surface like an eggshell.

Screen shot 9.8 Lava flows on the Moon.

The drawings, however, became particularly motivating for the students when they were creating the artwork for an animation. Their class teacher saw this as one of the most important aspects of the learning because they needed to know the animation sequence in detail for it to work: *'To do the animation they really had to internalise what they were doing and writing about. The conceptual understanding had to be really there'.* The students themselves saw animation as a useful way of communicating their ideas. One of the boys said: *'If you've got it in your book, the teacher will say "so what's going on here then?", but on the computer she can see exactly what's happening'.* The students also felt that it was the animation that really drew the audience in, as one of the girls said:

> *People like to see what's going on. People like to press buttons. People like to just muck about with the buttons to see more animation. It's like a cartoon, especially children like cartoons.*

After the piece was completed, the students showed their work to a group of adults. One adult asked the group about their animation of the phases of the Moon. The question had been about the practicalities of computer animation, but rather than answering how they made the animation, one student launched into an explanation of the science: *'well, when you see a crescent moon in the sky . . .'* As the same student later said to me about the project: *'You're learning science and get to learn to do animations like learning two things at once'*. Indeed, the fact that the students were using computer animation as a tool in clarifying the science, made it clear how effective that can be.

Example 2: Animation to develop scientific ideas

Project title:	*The Periodic Table*
Project focus:	Reactions of the Periodic Table
Curriculum area:	Science
Age group:	Year-9 (13 and 14 year olds)
Group structure:	Pairs
Location:	Two computers on trolleys at the side of the science lab wheeled in for the project
Time:	One hour a week for 7 weeks

Each week two pairs of students worked at the computers animating and describing reactions of different elements in the Periodic Table. Some pairs worked on more than one element, sometimes an element took more than a week and was contributed to by more than one pair of students. The science had already been studied in class, and students used notes from their exercise books to help them. Where necessary students found additional information in textbooks or by asking their science teacher. By the end of the project the whole class had taken part, using animation, text, images and sound. Each week, before starting their own work, the students looked back at the animations other students had done, giving them ideas and a standard to live up to. An image of the Periodic Table served as a menu screen, which linked the symbol for the element to the screen containing animation and information about that element. One student was concerned that people may not know the element by its chemical symbol, so she recorded her voice saying the name of the element on each box of the Periodic Table diagram.

Group 1 metals   Two girls made computer animations of how the group 1 metals, lithium, sodium and potassium, reacted when dropped in water (see Screen shot 9.9). They had seen the teacher demonstrating the reactions in the lab and had written them up in their books. On the computer they carefully drew the apparatus and animated lithium fizzing, sodium exploding with an orange flame and a larger explosion for potassium with a purple flame – a moving version of what they had already drawn in their exercise books. As there was still time in the lesson, they were asked what they thought would happen if rubidium, the next group 1 metal, was dropped into water. This had not been demonstrated in class, and the students had not considered what the reaction would be. After an amount of discussion they realised that there was a sequence to the violence of the reactions and that rubidium may make an even bigger explosion. After checking this out they animated rubidium with a big explosion cracking the glass beaker and a voice-over that explained: *'You might notice that when you go down the Periodic Table the explosion gets bigger and bigger when reacting with water'*.

Their science teacher was delighted with the process because it had produced an extension to the original learning: *'They predicted and showed what would happen with an element they'd never come across in their lives'*, he said. This was an important and difficult idea that the students had grasped. *'Using IT makes them so enthusiastic and much more willing to make that sort of jump than in class'*, he added.

Screen shot 9.9 Four-screen animation of sodium reacting with water.

Helium   Students had found in their study that helium is lighter than air. They were not sure how to present this as a moving image because helium cannot be seen. They considered a fairground with helium balloons that started flying away, but did not find the idea clear enough because it could simply be the wind. Their eventual animation showed a person holding a large helium balloon and being pulled up into the sky. Their science teacher added: *'It wasn't real but it got the idea across'*, which was, indeed, what the boys were trying to do.

Oxygen   To show how oxygen re-lights a glowing splint, two boys sung a rap in counterpoint to their animation of the splint relighting: *'The splint is now on fire! The splint is now on fire!'*

Copper   The students working on copper animated a coin turning black when heated. However they were not pleased with their first attempt as they found it hard to show the colour changing slowly. On their second attempt they animated their copper coin to turn to shades of grey to denote the time it took to do it. They were still not entirely pleased at the end of the lesson, but had to leave it unperfected as time had run out (see Screen shot 9.10).

The atom   This pair of students explained in pictures and text what an atom is and animated the electrons whizzing round the nucleus. They took a long time to get the animation exactly right because they were animating three electrons all going round in separate orbits at the same time, as shown in Screen shot 9.11. They had to re-do it a number of times before they were satisfied, but were very proud of the end result. Again the science teacher felt that *'it was a difficult idea and they made a movie out of it. It helped them to understand what was going on'*.

The noble gases   As the presentation the students were making was about the reactions of elements in the Periodic Table, there was nothing to animate for the inert or noble gases. A group of girls decided that as people may not know this in advance they should

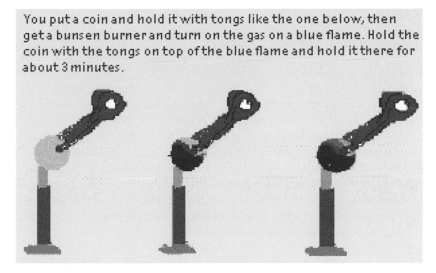

You put a coin and hold it with tongs like the one below, then get a bunsen burner and turn on the gas on a blue flame. Hold the coin with the tongs on top of the blue flame and hold it there for about 3 minutes.

Screen shot 9.10   Three-screen animation of copper changing colour.

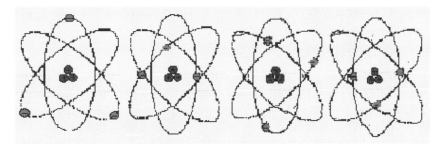

Screen shot 9.11   Four-screen animation of an atom.

be allowed to click on the noble gases to see what reaction would take place. They produced a voice-over in unison, '*We are the Noble Gases and we don't react with anything*'.

The science teacher was very keen on the outcomes. He stressed the class's enthusiasm and pride in their work. They stayed in at break and showed each other and replayed their animations. '*I was amazed at the quality of the work produced*', he admitted, '*better than in a regular class!*'

These two examples have focused on animation and how the moving image contributed to students' understanding and development. The combination of sound, still images and text provided the main elements to these pieces, which in themselves encouraged the students to research correct information. The enthusiasm engendered by the computers helped the students learn the science, with multimedia authoring being the vehicle to reinforce and develop the students' understanding of the subject.

In practice . . .

1. Teaching technical skills

In the process of a multimedia authoring project there are a variety of technical skills that will need to be taught. There are aspects of the particular authoring program being used, such as how to import images, how to create text areas and how to link screens together. There are also more general computer skills such as how to use a scanner, how to link up a digital camera and how to save the piece on to disk or into the right part of the school network. The students may come to your class already knowing some of these but, if not, short 15 or 20 minute watch and talk sessions followed by a practice period are the most useful. Students will not be able to learn a whole program in one go, and as they learn more, they will be able to find out more by themselves. For subsequent projects when students know the basics of the software, the time can be spent on discussions of more complex interactive features and multimedia concepts.

As a teacher, you will need to be confident with the software, but you do not need to know it inside out. The students will pick things up; you should nurture class experts in different aspects of computer work and make links with other teachers in the school who may be able to troubleshoot. Make sure that you have a simple manual for the software you are using.

2. Collecting information

For a multimedia authoring project students may need to research from books in libraries, CD ROMs and the Internet; discuss ideas with teachers, parents and other students; interview and record people; and photograph people, places or objects. In order to do this they will need to learn skills in collecting information such as how to summarise, take notes, use manual or electronic searches, ask questions in interviews, compose photographs and decide which bits of information are relevant. Some of these skills may need direct teaching, some could be taught as the need arises and some they may already know.

Although students may know what they want to collect, they can easily change their minds on account of what they have already found out, making information collection an ongoing process. The information will need to be collected in the different media and because the pieces are not yet put together, they will look incomplete individually.

Images

Images can be produced in different ways:

*   Computer drawn   Pictures can be drawn or painted straight on to the screen with the mouse – the tiger in Screen shot 9.12 has been created in this way. Computer drawing takes time and care; different software will offer different tools and colour palettes to draw with. Students often complain that it is difficult to draw straight on to the computer, and it does indeed take time to become proficient and to get

Screen shot 9.12 Image of a tiger drawn straight on to the screen using a mouse.

the image exactly as you want it. However these same students produce beautiful images which can be as engaging and full of character as any other artwork.

- Scanned images   Pictures can be created off the computer and scanned in. This gives much more scope to use different textures, watercolours, crayons, pencils, ink, wax etching, and so on. All scan on to the screen to great effect. Images do not need to be flat to be scanned on to the computer. Shells, sand and stones can be collected and used, as can coins, a piece of jewellery, or even your hand.
- Photographs   Photographs can be put on to the computer in three ways:

    i A digital camera stores images electronically and is then connected to the computer and displayed on the screen (see Plate 9.1).
    ii A regular camera can be used to take pictures which are then developed on to a photo CD ROM.
    iii Photographs can, of course, also be scanned on to the computer.

They can be manipulated to include just the parts required, or changed to add a different colour, time of day, or character. One class photographed a ladybird through a magnifying glass to add to their branching multimedia piece called *What am I?* Another class made a photographic montage of a Tudor domestic scene. They used three photographs taken on a class visit to a local Tudor house. Two photographs were of a Tudor fireplace in a kitchen with one of the students dressed in character. The third was a picture of a pot. First they fixed the two kitchen pictures together to give a wider view, they then reduced the size of the pot and cut and pasted it on to the fireplace (see Screen shot 5 in the colour section between pp. 92 and 93). Another school working on a geography piece used aerial views of the area taken from a helicopter, to complement their own photographs from their 7-year-old viewpoint. Satellite images are available on the Internet. Old pictures, postcards and holiday snaps are all good material. If photographs from books or the internet are used, you need to be aware of copyright if the work is going to be put on to a website or CD ROM for wider distribution than the school.

Plate 9.1 Students taking photographs of a model rainforest with a digital camera.

Examples of images are shown in the colour Screen shots between pp. 92 and 93 and on the CD ROM.

- Clipart   Students like to use clipart because it is professional looking and clear. It is helpful to use clipart as a way of teaching how to import and manipulate images. However, take care with computer generated graphics, patterns or animations, as the work tends to look fairly bland, and does not contain the character that shines through students' own artwork.

Animations

Animations can run on one screen or be used as a transition between screens. They can be drawn straight on to the computer or off the computer. In order to get the animation right, the process needs to be researched. For example, in looking at how animals move students might watch a video or CD ROM where they can slow down the action or freeze it frame by frame. They can then draw out the sequence of the animations before transferring it on to the computer. Photographic animation can be particularly effective – animating a number of photographs of the sea can make the waves flow, and taking images of a view at different parts of the day can create the feeling of time going by. A class working with a dancer on zero gravity looked at how people would move in space. One student wanted to show how, if twirled, someone could roll round and round. To do this she drew four pictures of her friend from different angles and sequenced them one after the other to show the student rolling. Examples of animations are shown on the CD ROM.

Text

Most text can be written straight on to the computer, however if there is only one computer at the side of the classroom, it is a shame to use it as a glorified typewriter, especially as students often take time to type in their text. It is possible to buy cheap, light, hand-held text processors which can be used in class (as shown in Plate 9.2) or carried on field trips, and the text can be transferred electronically on to the computer. Students will want to make choices about text colour and font. If it is a whole class piece, changing fonts every page can be irritating and it may be worthwhile to make a class decision on these aspects of the design. If the work is going to go on to another computer that does not have the font the students have used, the computer will automatically choose a different font, and it might not look as good as the original work. It is sensible to use a common font such as Times or Helvetica. Text, however, does not always need to be typed – handwritten text can be scanned in for effect.

Plate 9.2 A student using a portable text processor as part of general classroom activity.

In writing out information, students should take into consideration:

- Copyright.
- Audience.
- Truth. People's words can be twisted or quoted out of context. There are ethical issues here. With interviews, checking back with the person interviewed is good practice.

Sound

Sound will need to be recorded either straight on to the computer or taped. When recording speach, it is better for students to think of the ideas and say them rather than reading text, because that can sound stilted. A Viking story included dialogue between people which the students recorded in the classroom on the computer as a role play (see Screen shot 9.13). They tried it two or three times before they were satisfied. Although it was a fairly noisy classroom, they thought that it gave the atmosphere of a ship! Students can also be encouraged to make up original songs which they can rehearse and record. Sound effects may need to be recorded in situ with tape recorders. For example, one school made a multimedia piece about improvements to their local area, including Hackney marshes. They recorded geese and other birds, and lots of splashing about in mud, on to a small tape recorder and then transferred this on to the computer to create a good atmospheric effect.

Screen shot 9.13 Clicking on the buttons produces dialogue between the captain and the children.

Video

Although video looks great on the screen and can be simple to record, getting it on to the computer and editing it is extremely time consuming. It is difficult to fit into curriculum time and would be a better project for an after-school club. If video is going to be used for a curriculum project, make sure that enough time is put aside to edit it and there are some students who are keen to do it. The computer you use will need a video card and editing software, although some multimedia machines may come with them already installed. It is also possible to use ready made videos.

3. Linking it all together

The map of the multimedia presentation shows how the screens will link together. For younger students, the teacher may want to carry out the linking process, but this should be done in front of the class so that they can see what is happening. Other students should link the screens together themselves as this can increase their sense of how pieces of information connect to each other. This can be done in three ways.

- The blank screens can be linked together into a structure before the information is put on. This will enable the students to move easily between the screens as the navigation routes will already be in place. This will work if the navigation is solely in the form of buttons in the corner of the screen, but not if the links are on the images or on the words as hypertext because these images and words will need to be on the screen for it to link up. A way round this is to put prototype images and text on the screen.
- A second option is that the links are made as the screens are completed, so the student can see that the information is all on the screen as required and can add the buttons or hypertext links. The problem with this method is that although the screen to be linked *from* may be completed, it may not yet have anywhere to link *to*. If students are working on the same project at a number of computers, screens will not be accessible until they are transferred on to the same computer. This problem is solved if the school works with an intranet.
- The third method is to work on all the screens without adding any links, and only add the links when the screens are completed.

Realistically, students tend to use a mixture of these methods. They may begin by working on individual screens, but as soon as two screens to be linked together are completed, they are likely to want to make that link because it feels exciting and looks good. The most sensible route is to follow this course: encourage students to gather a certain amount of information and to begin linking when they can, leaving some of the links until the end if they are more complex. Linking as they go may give students a sense of the associative capabilities of multimedia authoring.

If the students are using the plans they have made, they will not have trouble working out which screen should link to which, and joining the piece together should be a fairly simple procedure. The plans, however, were made at the beginning of the project, and information gathered since then may have made the students rethink the way they had intended linking the piece up. Students may have collected extra information that was not in their original plans at all but they want to use. They may want to make the piece more interactive or add a new feature but not know where. All these are common elements that the students have to deal with and it is simpler to change the plans on paper first before they add the new parts on the computer.

Given the busy school schedule, it is always possible that plans get lost, are incomplete, are not completely agreed, are left at home, the person who has it is not at school that day or even that the students did not properly plan the piece in the first place. These difficulties could be pre-empted by making copies of the plans and ensuring early on that plans are in place before any computer work begins.

The final part of a whole class project will mean linking together the different stacks from different groups. If the class is working together at one computer, it is fairly straightforward. If students are working on a network they can put all their work into one user area to be linked together. If they are using two or three standalone computers, some stacks will need to be transferred by disk on to one machine.

Collecting and linking tips

- Do teach technical skills, but encourage students who pick them up quickly to become experts and help others.
- Using a variety of images is effective, some computer drawn, some scanned and some photographs.
- When creating artwork for scanning, encourage students to use a variety of textures. It adds depth to the screen.
- If you cannot get silence in a busy classroom to record sound, record it anyway.
- Only use video (even pre-recorded) if you have lots of time.
- Be aware of copyright if the work is going on to a website or CD ROM.
- When linking two screens, transitions can be created so that one screen dissolves into the next. There will be many possible transitions on offer and students will want to use all of them. However using different transitions for each screen can be irritating for the audience, and consistent transitions look better. If there is a menu screen, there could be one transition to leave the screen and a different one to return.
- The user will need to know where to click to move to the next screen. In web authoring hypertext is shown by the colour of the text or small icons. If there are to be invisible buttons over parts of an image there will need to be instructions explaining where to click.
- In a whole class project it is useful to designate a pair of students to be responsible for making sure the final links are made between different groups' work, pulling the piece together as a workable whole. This may well need to be done with the teacher's help.

Checklist

- Collect information, remembering it is an integrated medium.
- Scan images, add sounds, complete the screens.
- Link the piece together.

Chapter 10

Receiving and responding to critical feedback

Thinking about . . .

By the time the completed piece is linked together, it is easy to think that the project is finished and there is no more to do. However this will be missing out an important element of the work which will extend students' critical awareness around their own compositions. Throughout the project the students have been asked to think about the intended audience by making the pieces easy to understand, as clear as possible and attractive to look at. They have had to consider interactivity by designing game features and giving the user control and choice. The thoughts about audience response, however, were fairly abstract. Their classmates may have commented on aspects of the presentations during the process, but this was criticism of an unfinished piece which they themselves may have been involved with as co-authors. At this stage in the process, where seemingly all is finished, students need to set out to test their presentation with an outside audience who are unfamiliar with the project. This is to ascertain both whether their piece works adequately and whether their concepts of audience were accurate.

Before this process begins there may be an emotional barrier to overcome. If it is a whole group project, it may be the first time students in the class have seen the completed piece linked together, and this can be very effective and exciting as the disparate parts different groups have worked on become one. Although this is only the first draft of the whole piece, it is a second or third draft of individual screens and is the product of all the work and thought and discussions of many hours over a substantial period of time. Having worked hard, students will rightly feel a sense of pride in their piece and a feeling of ownership. If the presentations are a number of small group projects, it will also be the first time that the work has come together as a whole presentation. Students will feel attached to their pieces and this attachment needs to be dealt with carefully so that they are not incapable of hearing criticism and thus making changes.

Although this stage of responding to criticism is crucial and students can find it useful, it is also difficult, as American research of three separate studies of multimedia authoring attests. One group of researchers (Lehrer *et al*. 1994) worked with 9th-grade students (14 and 15 year olds) on making presentations of American history for their peers. In their evaluations only 15 per cent of the students ranked audience as an important aspect of this work. The students rarely asked for feedback from other students and were not happy to act on criticism, indeed, they would rigidly argue their case. Some students did alter their pieces after they had heard the criticism, but only by adding some navigation links so that the piece physically worked. The researchers claimed that: 'the students apparently thought that their inner audience and reactions from other members of their team made the test afforded by a real audience less important and perhaps trivial' (p. 241). A second study (Liu and Rutledge 1997), working with 15 and 16 year olds, found that the students who were making programs in history and science for 5 year olds had a strong sense of audience, but only acted on criticism if they agreed with it. The third study (Kafai *et al.* 1997) was of 5th- and 6th-grade students (10–12 year olds) working in science. The researchers found that the students were not very aware of their users and found it difficult to take other perspectives into account. When they did have a sample audience, rather than letting the audience use the piece themselves, the authors played it for them. These findings point to some of the difficulties students have in maintaining a sense of perspective about their work.

To avoid student defensiveness to criticism of their work, audience critical feedback needs to be approached in a positive and sensitive way. The students must understand that this stage is not an examination that needs to be passed, and the audience role is not only to criticise, but that this stage is one of the most useful parts of their project development, which would be an integrated part of any professional software design project. Just as it has been important to be up front and transparent about the process the students are going through at other stages of the project, here it is equally important. The more the students can see audience reaction as a vital part of helping them to achieve their goals, the less they will need to feel defensive about criticism.

Example 1: Feedback from another class

Project title: *The electricity line*
Project focus: What is electricity, where is it found and dangers
Curriculum area: Science
Age group: Year 5 (age 9–10)
Group structure: Whole class, small groups, pairs and individuals
Location: Large computer room with space
Time: Two hours a week for 8 weeks

This case study will describe the final afternoon session of this project, when the vast majority of the work had been completed. The idea was to show the almost completed version to members of a year-6 class (10–11 year olds) to get critical feedback.

The class had worked in groups, and each group had completed a section of the final piece. The teacher had linked all of these sections into one larger format which was shown to the class. Although they had seen a little of each other's work, this was the first time they had seen the whole piece together. The general enthusiasm and excitement at seeing the presentation was followed by a class briefing on what was to happen that afternoon. The teacher explained that the class would be split into four groups and each group would observe a few members of a year-6 class using their piece. The authors should watch how the older students used the piece, where they got stuck, where they needed help, and what they said to each other while they were looking at it (see Plate 10.1). The authors were told to sit silently and watch – they were not to tell the year-6 class where to click because if the users did not know what to do, the authors

Plate 10.1 The authors watching the critics looking at their piece.

needed to find out now so that they could make changes. They would get the chance to hear feedback and ask their own questions.

The year-6 class were also given a briefing before they came into the computer room. They were told that they were to see an almost complete piece of science work made by the year-5 class and that they could help them by 'playing' the electricity game and giving feedback on what things they liked and did not like about it and what they thought was interesting or they would like to know more about. They were also told that they would have the opportunity to ask the authors questions after they had spent time using the piece.

In the computer room four computers had the program up on the screens. Four year-6 students sat in front of each machine and the year-5 class were sitting or standing and watching them. The year-6 class were given a little over ten minutes to view the piece. They were very eager to see it and gave lots of (*'this is wicked!'*) positive feedback. During this time the authors watched (see Plate 10.2). Some complained they could not see, one complained that one of the authors had told one of the critics where to click. One girl who particularly liked her voice-over when you clicked on a supermarket till was upset that they had been on that screen and not clicked on the till. One observing group were incensed that the boys at the computer were just clicking through the piece without reading any of the writing. A girl in this group called me over to tell me that she was going to ask them what experiment Franklin did to find out about electricity because they would not know as they had not read the text. An all girls group moved through the piece much more slowly and read everything. They turned round at one point to their observing authors and asked: *'how do you go back?'*, but before answering another girl had suggested: *'press the time machine'*.

After ten minutes the students were brought back together and the feedback session began, with each group of critics in turn saying one thing they liked about the piece. Three of the groups described different bits of animation and sound. One group said

Plate 10.2 The authors sitting at a distance from the critics, as they were so excited and enthusiastic it was the only way to stop them jumping in to tell the critics what to do.

they liked having choices about where to go. None of the groups mentioned anything about the science content. The critics could then ask the authors one question about the piece. These questions were all technical, how did you do X. The authors were eager to answer, but came out with such technical details (*'first you click on objects and go to add a button and then you choose the right one and then you . . .'*), that the year-6 class, not knowing the software, did not understand.

The authors then had the chance to ask questions of the group of critics they had observed. The first group asked their critics: *'What did Benjamin Franklin do to carry out his experiments?'* When blank looks came from the boys' group who had not read the text, the authors moaned that they had not been reading it and proceeded to tell them about Franklin flying a kite in a storm. The next question was asked to the girls' group who had read the text assiduously: *'how do traffic lights work?'* Again, they did not know the answer; they admitted seeing the card and reading it, but could not remember. At this point the authors were a little unsettled. The class teacher suggested that the year-6 class had only had ten minutes to look at the piece so had to read through it fast. With a bold leading question he asked the year-6 class whether, given more time, such as having the CD ROM in their classroom, they would go through it in more detail. This was generally agreed.

Only at this stage were the critics asked for things they did not understand or that they felt needed improvement. One girl said that some of the text was blurry but could not remember where. Others made small comments for improvement about particular parts, but had few negative comments. It was important that the positive feedback had come first.

After the year-6 class had left, the authors had a discussion about the points that were brought up. A number of students were concerned that the year-6 class were not learning the science because they were not reading the text. One student suggested a comparison: *'you know how some people get a book and look at the pictures and then go back and read it'*. The class began to come to terms with this idea but would have needed more time to really respond to these worries and change the text accordingly. Certainly the class had not anticipated how little their text, that they worked so hard at, would be read. The class were keen to discover where the 'blurry writing' was, and went through the piece until they found it and changed it. There were not many changes needed, but the process of getting the criticism and dealing with it had been important. It appeared to make the students view their work in a different way; the audience had become a reality. The feedback session was structured slowly and carefully and it seemed to give the whole class a sense of how the piece belonged to all of them. At one point the teacher made remarks using the word 'criticism'. This startled a few students as the word 'feedback' had been used previously, and the 'criticism' had negative connotations for them. This feedback session would make an ideal starting point for their next multimedia authoring project, taking these criticisms into consideration.

Example 2: Responding to peer criticism

Project title:	*Genetically modified food*
Project focus:	How foods are genetically modified, the scientific and societal implications.
Curriculum area:	Science
Age group:	Year 10 (age 14–15), girls school
Group structure:	Whole class project working in pairs
Location:	Computer workshop, one computer per pair and desk space for off-computer work
Time:	Six classes over three weeks. Total time 8 hours

Being short of curriculum time this class did not test their piece with a sample audience. They did, however, give each other feedback and this case study describes that feedback. The class had been working in pairs at different computers and were into the last session of completing their pieces. They had not shared their work before this point, so the computer presentations were new to them, although some of the science was familiar. Each pair went to look at the work of their neighbouring pair before all four students sat in front of first one of the computers and then the other, and gave their comments and feedback.

Two student critics were looking at a presentation on cheese. The front cover showed an animation of two pieces of cheese waving to each other. They were immediately impressed and made exuberant comments, loud enough to be heard by the others who looked over:

Critic 1: *Oh my God, that was good.*
Critic 2: *It waves.*
Critic 1: *Oh, ours doesn't wave.*

They then went on to read through the text. The group had written in text boxes and the critics were concerned because they as users could change the text. These two students had found out in their own work that they could make text boxes 'read-only' so that they could not be changed by a user. They considered making the cheese presentation 'read-only' too, but, on their teacher's advice, decided to suggest this to the authors rather than do it for them. When giving feedback to the cheese authors the critics were very enthusiastic:

Critic 1:   The way you wrote it is simple and nice and the design is good.
Critic 2:   We really really liked yours. The cheese waving at us.

They also mentioned the 'read-only' possibilities.

After the critics had gone back to work on their own piece, one of the authors told me that she was pleased that the critics had liked the waving bit because she had thought it was rubbish! They had not understood what 'read-only' meant and were happy to ignore it, however, with some prodding they asked their critics to show them the technical details. In their final evaluation of the piece the cheese authors wrote that it had been useful to get the critical feedback as it gave them a chance to 'alter and improve' their piece. However this was obviously a theoretical point of view because when asked specifically whether they did change their piece, they replied that they did not because: 'there was less time left and it was only one person's criticism. Most people liked it'.

Another pair of critics were looking at a piece on strawberries. Two screens into the piece they got stuck because they did not know where to click on the screen and after trying everywhere and not finding anything did not know what to do to move on. In discussion, the authors told them that there was an automatic timer that moved through the pages and that there would be a voice-over keeping people interested so there did not need to be anywhere to click. The critics were not happy with that because they had not known they should just wait, and suggested the authors could write text telling people to wait. The authors complied with this suggestion (see Screen shot 10.1). In evaluation one author wrote: 'we did change our piece in order to enable the readers to have a better understanding of what we were trying to convey'.

A third pair of critics were looking at a piece on organic farming, but the author did not want their criticism. Her partner was absent from school, she felt that she had finished and did not want to change anything. Her critics suggested that she had too much writing on one page and that she could turn some of it into a voice-over explanation. The author looked sulky throughout this exchange, and after the critics went she left her piece and wandered around the classroom watching other students work. She did not change anything. In her evaluation sheet she said that feedback was useful as classmates 'added ideas to make it better', however, she did admit that she did not act on this criticism.

In this project it was difficult for the authors to accept criticism from their peers, and although they all wrote about the importance of feedback in evaluation, few of them acted on it. This may have been because they already saw the piece as finished. Criticism from their partner, peers and teachers was received much more readily in the middle of the project.

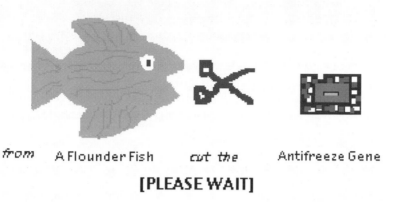

Screen shot 10.1 The changed screen on the science behind GM strawberries.

In practice . . .

Throughout the project students should have been getting feedback on their pieces in progress from their group, their classmates, their teacher, and anyone passing on an informal basis. This feedback should have sparked discussion and may have altered the wording of their pieces, navigation routes and the interactivity. Some of this feedback could have been part of a general class activity where groups took turns to view each other's work, reporting back to the group concerned or to the whole class. However this informal criticism has been structured, it is important that there has been ongoing sharing and criticism, and that although the sample audience may be the first people to see the whole piece, this is not the first time students have let their work be seen at all.

1. Choosing a sample audience

It is useful if the sample audience is as close to the real thing as possible, but this is not necessarily easy to arrange. If it cannot be precise, the students will have to consider how to find a representative audience for this situation. There are two aspects for the students to bear in mind when they make this decision.

- The people in the audience If the intended audience is the reception class of their school or the local primary school then there is no problem, they can trial the piece in school. If the intended audience is people who walk into a museum, it is not so simple. The students will know that the audience will have an interest in seeing the museum, but it may be hard to find people fitting the description. If the piece is a website the audience may be unknown. Although the trial will most probably not be perfect, a good degree of match would be useful.
- The context of viewing If the multimedia presentation is for another class to use when studying, for example, plate tectonics in geography, it can be trialled in another geography classroom but will be unlikely to fit in with the current geography context in that class, and the students may not have done the background work that would be assumed when the piece is to be used. If the presentation is for a museum, they may not be able to go to the museum to trial it. If the presentation is to be shown on a website, people may view it from a library or from their own homes, not a classroom setting.

These issues have an effect, because although you could trial a presentation with the right age group, they may not have the necessary background information or be in the right context. However, these variables do not need to be a problem. If year-7 students require background information for the piece, it can be trialled with experts in year 8 who know the subject. It is likely that context cannot be accommodated, but it should be borne in mind by the students when they are considering who the audience should be. As the sample will be close rather than precise, the piece could be trialled with a couple of different groups of people – one group who will be able to view the subject matter critically and another group who will be able to ascertain if the interactivity works well.

2. The audience feedback

Students might have to be reminded that their completed piece is a first draft. They may not need to make any large revisions, but they may need to do some, and this is a stage, not where they are being judged, but where they are going to observe and monitor the audience using their piece and learn from them. The perspective the students need is that the audience are doing them a favour by finding any glitches, lack of clarity, parts that they do not understand, missing buttons or animations that do not run before they put the piece into the public domain. They are also doing them a favour because the authors will have the opportunity to critically watch the audience using their piece and notice how they use it. They will be the audience for the audience and this is an active role. So there are two jobs in this phase.

The audience

The audience's job is to look through the piece and make any comments that they think about it, whether, positive, negative or neutral. They are to answer a number of questions:

- Is the text clear and easy to understand?
- Is it easy to navigate?
- What do they like about the design?
- What did they learn?
- What questions are they left with?
- What was interesting about it?
- How does the piece need to be improved?

The audience criticism needs to be about the way the piece communicates and how engaging it is. It may bring up issues of world view where individuals in the audience disagree with the author's perspective. This needs to be set aside to an extent as there will always be alternative interpretations of the subject, and the authors are the ones deciding on the slant of the piece.

The authors

It is the authors' job to watch the audience, to see how they 'play' the piece and to take notes of their observations. They are to answer a number of questions:

- Could the audience navigate well on their own or did they need to ask for help?
- Did they seem to enjoy the piece?
- Was there enough for them to do?
- Did they read the text?
- Were there any parts they missed out?
- Did they concentrate well?

They should also jot down any comments the audience make at this stage and any questions they want to ask them later.

This observation will give the authors information before the audience have given them specific feedback. This should, it is to be hoped, give the authors a sense of being in control and learning from this process.

This stage should be followed by a feedback session and discussion. This will work best if it is carefully structured so that the authors are not bombarded with information and do not get too much negative feedback. The audience can start by asking the authors any questions they have about the piece – whether it is about the subject matter, the way it worked, or how they made it. The authors should get a chance to explain some of what they have been doing. Using the criteria for observing the piece, the audience should then give their answers to the questions, which the authors should take note of. They can ask for clarification but not challenge or argue about any of the points raised at this stage.

The authors then have the opportunity to ask the audience questions about the piece, including factual questions to see if they have read the text. The authors will end up with a bank of critical information that they then need to talk about as a group when the audience have left. Again, perspective is paramount. Rather than defending the criticisms, the authors need to take them seriously, as if one of their own group had brought up that point. They do not need to take into account every criticism, but discuss and decide which ones are pertinent and need to be responded to. They should notice any criticisms that have been made by a number of people, and give them particular consideration, even if they do not agree with what has been said. They should also consider how the audience answered their questions and how engaged they were in viewing the piece, and discuss things that might need to be changed. This whole process should be time restricted and not take more than one further lesson to make any alterations. They may need to decide not to be perfectionists. It may also be possible to alter the piece after it has been completed. If it is a website, there can be an e-mail address for comments on the site that the students can act on; however, be aware that this will be an extra time commitment.

Feedback tips

- If audience has been emphasised frequently at different stages of the project, this stage should be exciting as it will be the culmination of that process.
- An audience of peers working in the classroom is almost always more critical than an outside audience.
- Planning a feedback session carefully will reap benefits so try not to just 'fit it in', but plan for it.
- Think about seating for setting up the session, so that the authors really become the audience to the critics, and are not tempted to join in.

Checklist

- Choose a sample audience.
- Let the audience of critics play while the authors watch and observe.
- The audience asks questions and gives feedback.
- The authors question the audience.
- Have a class discussion on how to respond to the feedback.
- Make changes to presentation if necessary.

Chapter 11

Student evaluation

Thinking about . . .

Student evaluation of a multimedia authoring project has two distinct purposes. The first is to make the students reflect on the process they have gone through in creating the multimedia presentation or website, and to take time to consider what they have learned from it. Younger students may *describe* the process, what they did and what they produced; older students should interpret and analyse the use of multimedia authoring in their learning and evaluate the end product against specific criteria. It is important that the students' evaluation leads them towards thinking about how they would improve the process next time, which should contribute to developing their understanding, raising standards and possibly developing new criteria for evaluation. The second purpose of student evaluation is to help the teacher with individual assessment. Teachers will assess the process and the product (as described in Chapter 12). However the project's outcome will be a group product where each individual's work will be an indivisible part of the whole. One student may have drawn a picture on one screen, collaborated on text for another and recorded sound for a third. Apart from it being difficult to pick out an individual's contribution, it would not be useful because collaboration may have been an important aspect of the quality of that student's work. Indeed, if students get a sense that they will be evaluated by the individual elements they produce in the final piece, this may set up a sense of competition which would be very unhelpful in terms of working as a group. The students' own evaluations of what they did as part of a group and how they contributed to it, as well as how they considered other aspects of the project, will give the teacher insight into each individual's understanding of the process.

The evaluation will need to be based on criteria that were acknowledged at the outset of the project (see Chapter 2), but also include any additional criteria that developed during the process of working on the piece. A useful way to begin an evaluation session is with a whole class discussion which can include an initial explanation of the process of evaluation. This should include a review of the criteria and general feedback from class members on how fully they felt these criteria were met. This should encourage students to think about the issues and remind them of some aspects they may have forgotten. It is difficult in a large group, however, for every student to get a turn to talk and for the teacher to assess students from this group discussion. It is more likely to be a useful precursor to a written evaluation. The openness of the preliminary discussion may help students to see the process of evaluation as a way of reflecting on what they have learned and on how they have learned it rather than as a test of their knowledge and memory.

Example 1: Mixed questions

Age: Year 9 (13 and 14 year olds)
Subject: Science

This class were given the evaluation form without any discussion and asked to complete it in class time. The form uses a mixture of open questions which give room for fuller answers, and multiple choice questions with an option for the students to write their own answers if the suggested answers did not fit.

---

1. **How did you plan your project?**

   Wrote information out for each screen ☐

   Drew plans of all screens showing links with arrows ☐

   Didn't plan project in advance ☐

   Other . . . .

   . . . .

   . . . .

2. **How did you work on your plan?**

   Together with your partner ☐

   Separately and shared ideas ☐

   On your own ☐

   Your partner planned it ☐

   Neither of you planned it ☐

   Other . . . .

   . . . .

   . . . .

3. **Who did you get most help from?**

   Your partner ☐

   One of the teachers ☐

Another student in the class ☐

Other . . . .

. . . .

. . . .

4. **What TWO things did you most enjoy about this project?**

. . . .

. . . .

. . . .

5. **How well did you and your partner work together?**

We worked very well together ☐

We both worked separately on different bits ☐

My partner did most of it him/herself ☐

We didn't work very well together ☐

Other . . . .

. . . .

. . . .

6. **What was the most difficult part of the project?**

. . . .

. . . .

. . . .

7. **How do you feel about using the program?**

Confident ☐

All right ☐

Not very confident ☐

Can't do it ☐

8. **What facts or ideas about the science work you were presenting really stick in your mind from the project?**

   . . . .

   . . . .

   . . . .

9. **Did you think about who was going to use the piece after you made it?**

   YES   ☐   NO   ☐

10. **If YES, who was the intended audience?**

   . . . .

   . . . .

   . . . .

11. **What did you have to take into consideration when thinking about this audience?**

   . . . .

   . . . .

   . . . .

12. **What are the THREE most important things to think about when making a multimedia game?**

   Plan it in advance   ☐   Produce good drawings   ☐

   Know the science well   ☐   Link the screens   ☐

   Write clear concise text   ☐   Consider who the audience will be ☐

   Get someone to try it out   ☐   Change parts if necessary   ☐

   Other . . . .

   . . . .

   . . . .

13. What did you NOT enjoy about the project?

. . . .

. . . .

. . . .

14. Would you like to do a project like this again?

In science?   YES ☐   NO ☐

In another subject?   YES ☐   NO ☐

Which one?

. . . .

. . . .

. . . .

15. What would you change next time?

. . . .

. . . .

. . . .

16. Any other comment.

. . . .

. . . .

. . . .

A few things became clear from this evaluation form. First, it gave the students a voice; the students were often honest in making negative comments as well as positive, many of them using the option 'Other' or 'Any other comments' to tell the teacher what they thought of how the project was run. For example, one girl who was annoyed at the class being told by the teacher to use a restricted colour palette in their artwork wrote under, 'What would you change next time?': 'We should have permission to use any facilities, every colour and background to make it more attractive'.

Other students wrote how much they enjoyed the project and would want to repeat it. One student wrote how she enjoyed filling in the questionnaire, and there is always one delightful student who thanks the teacher.

Second, the form highlighted areas where the whole class were unsure of the ideas. When asked who the audience for the piece was, there were many different answers, although most of them wrote: 'Our age', 'Schoolchildren', 'Our age or younger', there were also two responses of *'Anybody'* and one of *'People who care'*. This showed how this subject had not been adequately discussed with the students and is useful feedback to the teacher for consideration in the next multimedia project. Finally, in question 12, by far the most common answers were planning, considering audience and linking screens. Almost no one mentioned the science content. This may be because the students had understood that the project was a multimedia computer project and were focusing solely on that. This does cast doubt on using multiple choice options, as this type of question may make students think that there is a correct answer, and does not give them the opportunity to think for themselves about the important elements of the process they have just gone through. An open question may well have been better here.

Example 2: Open questions

Age: Year 10 (14 and 15 year olds)
Subject: Geography

At the beginning of the final lesson a whole class discussion considered design issues and how useful feedback had been. They were then given an evaluation form only focusing on these issues to complete for homework.

---

1. **In making a multimedia program, pictures, text, animation, sound and interactivity all combine.**

   Think of one screen that you worked on.

   Describe the screen . . . .

   . . . .

   . . . .

   Why was it effective? . . . .

   . . . .

   . . . .

   How did you make decisions about design? . . . .

   . . . .

   . . . .

Why did you decide that particular information should be written, which should be images, which animated, pop-up boxes, and so on? . . . .

. . . .

. . . .

2. **You were able to get feedback from teachers and classmates during the project.**

Has it been useful to get critical feedback from your classmates?

Yes/No

In what way/why not? . . . .

. . . .

. . . .

Did you change your piece because of criticism from classmates?

Yes/No

Why or why not? . . . .

. . . .

. . . .

Did you change your piece because of criticism from teachers?

Yes/No

Why or why not? . . . .

. . . .

. . . .

3. **Thinking about the project carefully, what do you feel you have learned from it in IT or geography or both?**

. . . .

. . . .

. . . .

This evaluation form only had open ended questions and produced a greater variety of responses than the previous form, and much more detailed feedback. Although students are able to give honest answers, there is always the possibility that they will write what they think the teacher wants to hear. This will need to be a consideration in any student evaluation. It was particularly useful to ask students to describe a screen before commenting on it because it made them focus clearly on one feature rather than making generalisations about the whole project. It is possible for the teacher to see how clearly students have understood the nature of multimedia from their use of language, as they take on the jargon of multimedia in their responses; for example, one girl explaining why her screen was effective wrote: *'The writing popped up when you dragged the mouse over it making it more interactive and giving more information, adding to the pictures'*.

Example 3: Oral questions

Age: Year 5 (9 and 10 year olds)
Subject: History

This class were not given these questions as an evaluation form. Instead there was a classroom discussion about the project immediately after it was completed, and it was not until the following week that the evaluation took place. The teacher read out each question to the class, and gave them time to write their responses, so that everyone was going through the process at the same rate. This may have been less flexible for students who needed more or less time, but the teacher wanted to be sure that every student understood the questions.

1. In what way is your multimedia presentation different to doing history in an exercise book?

2. Choose one screen you worked on that you are pleased with and describe what it looks like.

3. What do you like about it?

4. What did you have to do to make it?

5. What would the person using it have to do?

6. Who was the project for?

7. What did you need to think about so that they would be able to use the piece?

8. Was there anything you found difficult in the project? What was it?

9. Would you like to do a project like this again?

10. What would you change next time?

The responses varied in sophistication and understanding, and showed the students' positions in other areas, not just multimedia. For example, in answer to question one, one student wrote: 'Books are boring. In our game we have actions and more detail', whereas another carefully detailed: 'You click on start and then you go to another page and can choose where to go to, then you . . .' and a third explained that: 'A book can take you away into another world. With a computer you need to use a lot more concentration'.

How evaluation is set up will contribute to the quality of the responses. The first form got a response from everyone in the class because it was in class time, but some of them were completed very quickly, as the multiple choice options could be selected without too much thought. The second example, which the students did for homework, had a smaller response in that not everyone returned their forms, but the answers were detailed and thoughtful. The final form had a response from everyone in the class, and they were thoughtful responses. This was partly due to the initial discussion of the project but also due to the teacher being able to go round and help students consider the questions as they were answering them. These evaluation forms each tell the teacher different aspects of how the students are thinking about multimedia authoring in general and the project they have just completed in particular. As they are only a part of what could have been asked, teachers need to be clear about what they want to know before designing the form.

In practice . . .

A written evaluation can be given in the form of questions for students to answer in a questionnaire, or it can be a piece of narrative writing where certain questions are considered. Different styles will suit different ages and abilities. Care needs to be taken when asking questions. If they are too direct or jargon filled, the students might not understand them or might find them difficult to answer; however, it is important to incorporate jargon that was used, integrated and explained during the project. Some questions will require factual answers and some will be students' opinions. Some questions will help students focus on what they were doing and some will be specifically intended to help you assess them. As questions will need to be sensitive, age appropriate and relevant to the subject, they may need to take a roundabout route in getting at the information wanted. It would be useful to let students see the evaluation sheet early on in the project, so that they know what they are working towards. This will help make the process transparent and may reduce the sense of there being right and wrong answers. It will be helpful to the students to keep a diary throughout the project and this can be focused on a few of the areas that will be used in the final evaluation.

When designing evaluation forms do not try to cover too much. It is useful to have a mixture of questions, some requiring one-word answers, some asking for a word to be underlined or a number on a scale, and some requiring detailed written answers. The variety will make the evaluation sheet more accessible than solely text. This chapter gives sample questions under different headings, attempting to cover a wide range of possibilities which can be manipulated to create a personally tailored evaluation form to suit the particular project's criteria. This is not intended to be used as an evaluation sheet as it is much too long and covers a wide age range. The headings used here are relevant for the teacher who is preparing the student evaluation sheets, but are almost certainly not relevant for the students.

1. The multimedia authoring process

Purpose

- What was your piece about?
- What ideas did you want to get across?
- How did you decide what the purpose was?
- Did everyone agree? How did you decide if you did not agree?

Audience and interactivity

- Did you think about who was going to use the piece after you had finished it?
- Who is it for?
- What did you have to think about while you were making the piece to be sure that the audience would understand it?
- How did you make the piece like a game?
- When someone is using your piece, what will they have to do?
- What did you do if your idea did not work?
- What is interactivity?

- Did you change your piece after feedback from anyone? What did you do?
- What piece of feedback did you not respond to? Why?

Planning and non-linear environments

- Did you plan your project? When? How?
- Did you use your plans when you were working on the piece? If so, when?
- Did you change your plan at all? How?
- In what way was this project different to writing a project in your exercise book?
- How is a multimedia program different to a book?
- How did you decide what screen should link to what other screen?

Collecting information and design

- Did you do any research?
- How did you research?
- How did you know what to research?

In your project you used many different ways to communicate your ideas. You may have used text, pictures, animation, sound and video.

- What did you use?
- Which did you enjoy most?
- Was it difficult to decide which one to choose?
- How did you decide which one to use?
- When would you use a picture rather than some writing?
- Why would you add sound?
- What does animation add to your piece?
- Describe a screen that uses a number of different ways to get your ideas across.
- How did you make all the media combine on the screen?

The subject matter

You might want to ask factual, subject specific information. You might also want to ask:

- Have you used multimedia in this way in [subject] before?
- Did you enjoy making a multimedia presentation in [subject]? Why/why not?
- How was it different to the way you usually study [subject]?
- Would you like to work in this way again in [subject]?
- Would you like to work in this way again in another subject? Which one?

Working with others

- Who did you work with?
- Who did you get most help from?

- What help did you ask for?
- Did you help other people? What did you do?
- What do you need to think about when you're explaining something to someone?
- Did you discuss ideas with other students in your class/group?
- What did you discuss?
- Is it useful to discuss things? Why/why not?
- Do you like working in groups? Why/why not?
- What two things did you contribute to the group?

Technical skills

- Did you enjoy using [name of program]?
- Do you feel confident to make
  buttons
  text boxes
  animation?
- Could you explain how to use [name of program] to someone else? (specify aspects of the program)

Your feelings

- Did you enjoy the project? Why/why not?
- What was your favourite part?
- What did you not like?
- What did you find difficult?
- What would you do differently next time?

General

- What are the three most important things to think about when making a multimedia game?
- What advice would you give someone else who was doing a multimedia authoring project?

2. Evaluation of the final piece

- What was good about it?
- What was your favourite part?
- Did it work well? Explain.
- Which parts were interactive? (What did the audience have to do?)
- How did an audience respond?
- Does the user know what to do? How do they know?
- Is the information correct and easy to read?
- Is there a good mixture of text, pictures, sound and animation?
- Is it interesting? What in particular?
- Is it entertaining? What in particular?

Evaluation tips

- Do not give too many questions.
- Ask questions only if the answers will be useful for the students and yourself.
- You may want to write at the top of the form: *There are no right answers*.
- A pleasant looking evaluation sheet can be fun for the students.

Checklist

- Design and produce an evaluation session or evaluation form.
- Discuss issues of evaluation with the whole class.
- Help them work through the evaluation.

Chapter 12

Teacher assessment

Teacher assessment of a multimedia authoring project should be set against the same criteria as the student evaluation, which were defined at the beginning of the project. If there are extra criteria a teacher wants to add that the students are unaware of, this is possible, but it will give a different sort of result to the criteria the students are aware of.

The project needs to be assessed both on the process the students went through in creating the multimedia presentation and on the product, which is the multimedia presentation itself. In other subject areas such as drama, there is ongoing discussion about the relative importance of process and of product. If the process is where the majority of learning happens, is it important to assess the product? As the final product is often a public display, whether a play or a multimedia program, it is useful to assess how well it serves its intended purpose. Indeed, the way a multimedia presentation or website is structured shows certain aspects of the process and the students' understanding of the medium and how it works.

This does not make for straightforward assessment, however, because if the work has been done collaboratively in groups then the assessment needs to reflect that. Assessing the process can chart the development of each individual student around a range of criteria, but the completed multimedia presentation will be different because it is a group product. As mentioned in Chapter 11, it is pointless to try to dissect a piece for each individual's contribution because it was made as an integrated whole. Students' self-evaluation will help the teacher assess each individual by their understanding of the product.

Assessing the process

The assessment of the process will need to be an ongoing part of the project. There are many criteria that can be listed as important in assessment, most of which do not have a yes/no value that can be put on them, but can be considered part of a progression continuum. The skills and activities of the process of multimedia authoring can be split up in many ways. Here six areas are considered; audience and interactivity, non-linear environments, data collection and design, subject specific learning, working with others, and technical skills. An ability to create links may have a yes or no answer, but participating in group discussion and awareness of audience are on a continuum, with gradations of answers in between. This needs to be taken into account in terms of progression at different ages and levels of experience. At key stage 1 (up to age 7) you would not expect audience awareness to feature. By key stage 3 (11–14) it is essential.

This ongoing assessment can happen through observation, discussion with students and taking account of their written evaluations. When using the student evaluation, a word of caution; some answers may display a lack of clarity in the project setup rather than students not understanding a concept. For example, the year 9 class described in Chapter 11 who all gave different answers as to who the audience was, are an example of how this concept had not been adequately discussed in the first place, so there was no possibility of the students knowing who the audience was.

1. Audience and interactivity

The choice of who the audience is will affect how much the students need to take audience into consideration. This is shown in Figure 12.1. In writing for an unknown audience it will not be possible to be personal and the piece may need to be more generic. Writing for a younger age group in the school will bring in skills of needing to précis and simplify material and use age appropriate words, images and interactive elements. Useful assessment criteria are:

*   Awareness of audience the piece is being made for.
*   Knowledge of the purpose for the piece.
*   Understanding what interactivity is and how it relates to audience.
*   Ability to integrate interactive elements into the planning and presentation.

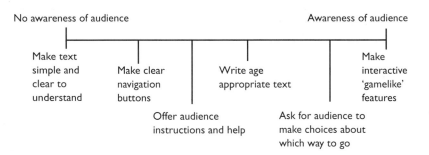

Figure 12.1 Progression route 1 – students' audience awareness.

2. Non-linear environments and planning

If students have had previous experience of hypermedia authoring this may change the entry level for assessment of this aspect. The understanding of non-linear environments can be judged by asking students questions and by considering the final plans of their pieces. Useful assessment criteria are:

*   Understanding the difference between linear and non-linear.
*   Ability to understand how paper plans relate to screen links.

The progression route for planning is shown in Figure 12.2.

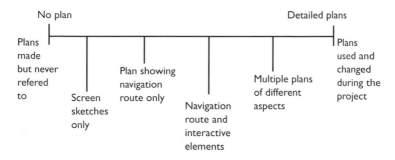

Figure 12.2 Progression route 2 – planning.

3. Data collection and design

As students get used to the mixture of media, the quality of their artwork, writing, sound elements and animations needs to be taken into consideration. If they can make integrated compositions, but the elements are of a very poor quality, this will not produce effective multimedia. Useful assessment criteria are:

- Awareness that multimedia uses a range of media to communicate ideas.
- Consideration of why one medium would be used in preference to another for a particular piece of information.
- Ability to use different media on an individual screen as integrated multimedia rather than annotated text.
- Ability to collect the data needed for individual screens.
- Consideration of clarity of text or sound
- Ability to produce quality work in the different media.

This progression route is shown in Figure 12.3.

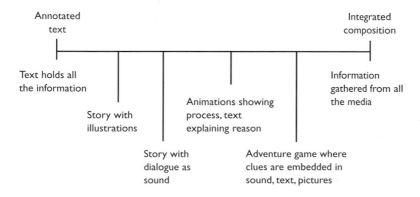

Figure 12.3 Progression route 3 – annotated text/integrated composition.

4. Subject matter

The subject matter itself may be assessed in whatever way it would generally be assessed. This part of the assessment is specifically concerned with relating the subject to the issues of hypermedia authoring. Useful assessment criteria are the ability to:

*   split information into manageable chunks
*   research from relevant sources
*   adapt the information researched to the audience
*   communicate the subject matter from their own point of view.

5. Working with others

Although individuals can make multimedia presentations on their own, this book is concerned with groups working together. Useful assessment criteria are the ability to:

*   participate in group discussion
*   work together with others in the group
*   hold an argument
*   listen to others
*   share computer work
*   help others in the group/class by listening to questions and responding
*   ask for help when needed from other students as well as teachers
*   explain an idea succinctly
*   demonstrate a technical aspect of the computer work
*   criticise in a constructive way
*   respond to criticism by changing work if necessary.

The progression route for collaboration is shown in Figure 12.4.

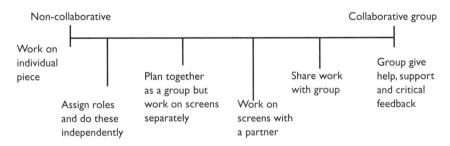

Figure 12.4 Progression route 4 – collaboration.

6. Technical skills

Technical skills are more like a tick list of what students are able and are not able to do. They are either able to add sound or not able to do so yet. It may be useful to have a middle category of 'are able to do with help'. The specific technical skills will depend on the software and hardware being used, and the prior expertise of the students.

Useful assessment criteria are:

- a growing knowledge of the software
- an attempt to find a way round technical problems as they arise;

and abilities to:

- add text and sound
- draft and redraft work
- make animations
- import and scan images and edit them on the screen
- use a digital camera
- create links between screens.

This is a fairly comprehensive but not exhaustive list of assessment criteria. It is important to remember that for any multimedia authoring project, it is unlikely that all of this will be a part of the assessment, and indeed it would be very time consuming if it were. It is more likely that one or two particular aspects will carry more weight than others, and some aspects will not be relevant. There are also likely to be some very specific criteria related to the subject that will need to be taken into account. These decisions should be made by the individual teacher with knowledge of the class and the nature of the project.

Evaluating the product

The teacher evaluation of the product, as discussed earlier, will not relate to individual students as it is a group product. This may be seen as problematic in terms of assessing individual students, however it can be viewed differently. The product evaluation can be seen as a good way to assess the success of group work. It can also be useful for teachers to move themselves on in terms of thinking about future projects.

The multimedia presentation should be assessed along a number of continua.

Audience viewing . . . . audience control
Annotated text . . . . integrated composition
Static . . . . interactive
Linear . . . . non-linear

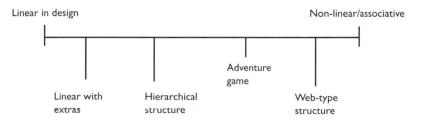

Figure 12.5 Progression route 5 – linear/associative.

The linear–non-linear continuum is shown in Figure 12.5. The following questions should also be asked:

> Does the piece do what it was intended to do?
> Is the piece pitched towards the right audience?
> Does it get ideas across well?
> Is it done with seriousness, humour, a mixture?
> Is the navigation consistent?
> Does the user know what to do?
> Is the information correct?
> Is there a good variety of different media?
> Is the piece in the authors' words?
> Are the authors critical of the information they use?
> Is the piece interactive?
> Is the factual information correct?
> Is it all linked together correctly?

Teacher reflection

Finally, as a teacher using multimedia authoring you might want to consider how the project went from different perspectives and ask yourself a few questions:

* Did the students learn as much about the subject as you wanted them too?
* If not, how could this be improved next time?
* Were they engaged in the subject in a different way from usual?
* Did you feel familiar enough with the software?
* If not, which particular aspects will you need to learn?
* Did you feel confident enough with general aspects of multimedia authoring, such as how to take audience into consideration and developing interactivity?

The work as a whole may reflect your confidence to this point in using multimedia authoring. In this sense it is useful to consider how you can move the class on and develop an increasingly sophisticated approach to multimedia or web authoring in the future, applying it to different curriculum areas in primary schools or different aspects of your subject in secondary schools.

Chapter 13

Infants making multimedia

Multimedia authoring is usually seen as a presentation medium for older students, however it can be used to good effect with young children too. One Hackney nursery school (3–4 year olds) makes multimedia stories about the children in the nursery. The teacher takes photographs of the students with a digital camera and transfers them into a multimedia authoring program. She then works with the students and they write a sentence together about the picture. The teacher animates the pictures of each child moving across the screen or jumping up and down to go with a recorded voice-over. These can then be accessed by the students clicking on photographs of themselves.

A reception class in another school (4–5 year olds) made a class album. This was at the beginning of the academic year in September and there was to be a second intake of students in January. Each child in the class drew two pictures. The first one was a self portrait and the second one was a picture of where they lived. The students told the teacher something about themselves which was typed on to the page of their portrait. Each student recorded their voice saying what they liked doing at home on to the second screen. On an opening screen the teacher reduced the portraits to make them all fit on together and linked the larger pictures and home pictures to this. This became a simple and effective class album (see Screen shot 13.1) where the new children coming in January could be introduced to the class and could add their own pictures.

Screen shot 13.1 Class album.

This may indeed not be multimedia authoring where the student is designing and planning and being the author of the whole piece, but it is a good start to understanding what multimedia is, and that it can be authored, or indeed co-authored. This chapter will look at two stories written by whole classes in years 1 and 2 (5–7 year olds). Both these stories and the class album described above can be seen in full on the CD ROM.

Example 1: *The Computer children*

Project focus:	Shape and story
Curriculum area:	Numeracy and literacy
Age group:	Year 1 (5–6 year olds)
Group structure:	Whole class, pairs and individual work
Location:	One computer at the side of the room
Time:	Three hours a week for 5 weeks

This began as a project on number and shape. The idea was for the children to make a counting game with triangles, squares, circles and rectangles where they made pictures with shapes. The user would have to count the numbers of different shapes in their pictures and choose the correct answer. The children would make the content for the piece, and the teacher, working with the children, would link up the screens and add the quiz element. It was to be a fairly small computer game where the students learning about shape would enjoy seeing the pictures they had made on the computer, and the game could then be used as a resource by the class. Essentially they were making it for themselves and whoever else would happen to come by. However, things did not go entirely as planned.

The project began with the students building models on their tables with different shapes of blocks or counters. Each table began with one shape, making models with only circles or rectangles or triangles before moving on to making models with more than one shape. Photographs were taken with a digital camera and were transferred on to the computer for the students to set up the counting game (see Screen shot 13.2).

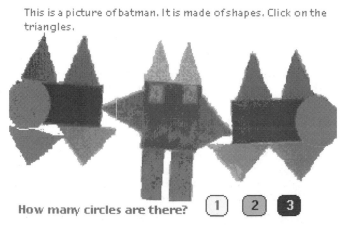

This is a picture of batman. It is made of shapes. Click on the triangles.

How many circles are there?   1   2   3

Screen shot 13.2   A shape sum for the counting game.

When the students got to this stage their teacher decided that as they were making pictures of things in the world (faces, Batman, houses and fire engines), the project needed a story to give it more relevance and to put the concept of shape into context. He set up a brainstorming session where the children thought of a story about a group of children in their class. They began with the idea that some of the class went to the park and fell into the pond. This produced many suggestions of what happened next (they found treasure, a shark chased them, they were pulled out on a rope, a submarine came to save them), and rather than choosing one, their teacher decided to use all the ideas and to have them as alternative endings. The submarine rescue is shown in Screen shot 13.3.

Screen shot 13.3 One of four multiple endings.

In pairs the class began drawing out the story straight on to the computer. Some of the students needed quite a lot of supervision as they were very varied in ability. There were some who could draw confidently, make text boxes and change colours. The teacher even claimed that if he had shown them how they might have been able to make buttons, although not create the links between screens. Other children had a lot of trouble controlling the mouse and were frustrated by not being able to draw a straight line or a circle in the place they wanted. For this reason the teacher put children of mixed abilities working together at the computer so that they could help each other. Working in pairs needed rules so that the more able child would not just take over from his or her partner. They were told that when working in pairs they had to take turns, one on the keyboard and one on the mouse. They could help each other by speaking, but not by taking the mouse away from the person using it, unless they were specifically asked. It was important that all the students contributed successfully to the piece, although some children would not have been able to do the work without help from their teacher, other children or other adults in the classroom. The help given to the students varied from a simple reminder of how to do something to guiding a student's hand to help them make the shape for their picture. All in all, the teacher said that he was 'amazed' at how well the pictures came out.

The children ended up with two computer stacks (files), one with a number of screens with shape pictures and sums, and one with the different screens of the storyline. This had been done gradually over a few weeks and every class member had had at least one turn at the computer. The screens of the story had been linked together along the way as they were simple moves between one screen and the next. The teacher finished off linking the alternative endings so that the story could now be used. The shape sums, however, needed to be linked in, so the children were asked to go through the story and find hidden shapes in the pictures they had drawn that were the same as those in their shape pictures. These would then be the link pictures to join up the story with the shape sums (see Screen shot 13.4). Their class teacher explained:

> Some were looking at the shark's fin and saying, 'that's a triangle'. There were loads of shapes – so as they were making the story they were thinking of shapes, and when they were reading through it when it was finished, they had to find them again.

Although the children did not add the buttons linking the story to the shape sums, they had found where they wanted these links to be.

One day Christine and Shaun put their heads through the hole for the CD ROM and then they crept away.

WATCH OUT. On this page and on other pages there are secret shapes. If you click on them you'll find out more. THERE ARE 4!!

Screen shot 13.4 Part of the storyline. Clicking on the computer links to a rectangle sum.

The pictures of characters in the story were students' self-portraits which they enjoyed looking at as they could point at their picture and say 'that's me'. After the piece was completed and linked together the whole class sat on the carpet looking at the computer to add sound to the different characters. The teacher did the mouse work and individual students came up to the computer to record their voices. The teacher described how the children loved doing the sounds, probably their favourite part:

> *they really wanted to do it, but when it came to it they were quite embarrassed, although most did it in the end. That was one of the most exciting bits for them because they were on it, not just their picture, but they could speak.*

One interesting aspect of the voices was that some of the children were too shy to speak on to the computer so other children did a voice-over for them. The class knew who everyone was on the piece and could recognise the voices, so if Harris had done the voice for Sean's character, the children would tell you: *'it's not Sean, it's Harris'*.

This association with the characters of themselves that they had created, gave the children a strong sense of ownership and feeling that the story was theirs. This was useful as their teacher explained: *'Because it was theirs, they quickly got very familiar with it and knew it inside out, and sometimes referred to it when talking about other stories'*. In fact, the teacher saw the development from an intended numeracy project to a literacy project as a vital aspect of the learning:

> *The main benefit they got from it [the project] was they learned about story structure, so afterwards in their writing their ideas were better. They got a feel for beginnings, incidents that happen, causes and effects. It wasn't necessarily that their written work had improved, just their way of thinking about stories.*

Indeed after the project was over when the children were asked to think of a story some of the students reverted back to 'falling into a pond' stories.

Example 2: Petsy

Project focus:	Stories
Curriculum area:	Literacy
Age group:	Year 2 (6–7 year olds)
Group structure:	Whole class, pairs and individual work
Location:	One computer at the side of the classroom
Time:	One morning a week for six weeks

This project was a literacy project inspired by BBC Television's 'Words and Pictures' programme for young children. The class were going to write a shared class story and look at rhyming words. Their story began with a playground fantasy where two of the children in the class found a strange animal in the playground and nobody knew what it was or where it came from. The students wanted to keep it but their teacher told them to find out first if it belonged to anyone (see Screen shot 13.5).

The teacher drew out a linear storyboard with boxes denoting the different screens. The students brainstormed where the animal could have come from. They began with some sensible suggestions such as the zoo or Hackney farm, but ran out of these until

They ran into the classroom, Nadege was carrying the animal. Mrs Pereira jumped with shock.

2 x 4 = 8
20 + 50 = 70

Screen shot 13.5 A story screen from *Petsy.*

someone suggested McDonald's and this was followed by an array of ideas from Marks and Spencer's in Mare Street to New York and Saturn. The teacher liked the class experience of working out the story together because everyone's ideas could then be used. As to the more outlandish ideas, the class teacher explained that after they made this piece they had done a science project to investigate where different animals came from, but when they were writing this story they did not know, so said the first things that came into their heads, Mare Street was near the school and Grace's mother had just been on a holiday to New York! However, as this animal was an alien creature, outlandish suggestions were pretty sensible. All these suggestions were incorporated into the story – Screen shot 13.6 shows one example.

The students drew pictures off the computer of these places and made collages with silver paper, felt, cotton wool, glitter and other materials. They were scanned in for them on another computer, put on to disk and brought back to their computer. They learned how to make buttons to add sound and they became the characters and the strange animal. Like the *Computer children* project, sound was a fascination to this class. They loved hearing their voices being played back and would click the characters over and over again to hear them. The sounds of the voices were full of expression and they particularly loved the grunts of the animal and their fancy voice imitation of their teacher, which made them laugh every time they played it.

When the story had been written, they went back through it and found one word on each page to rhyme with other words, and drew out these words with small images. On the 'ing' page as they were adding sounds, the student who said 'sing' sang it. This made all the students want to re-record their voices singing their words. Some 'ing' words are shown on Screen shot 13.7.

The computer work was made easier by a confident classroom assistant who helped the students with the technical side of the project. She described what situation might arise:

Nadesh and Matthew flew to New York to see if the strange animal lived there. When they got there, there were lots of people and lots of tall buildings, but no animals like Petsy. They asked the Statue of Liberty if she could help.

Click on her for her reply.

What animals live in the city?

Screen shot 13.6   New York – one of several paths through the story.

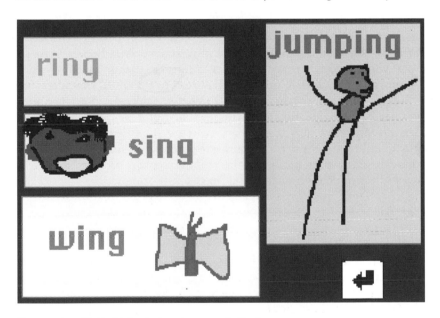

Screen shot 13.7   Linked rhyming words 'ing' page.

I wrote a lot down [how to use the program] *and re-read it to remind me. I had to learn a little quicker than the kids. Sometimes I couldn't get out of something and they'd say 'get out of it' and I'd say 'I don't know how to' and then I'd mess about with the buttons and all of a sudden you'd get out of it'.*

The students were taught how to copy and paste because characters from one screen would often appear in another. Although they began to get the concept of what copy and paste meant, they did not necessarily know exactly how to do it, but learning the concept may be cognitively more important at this stage than remembering the technical skills. The class teacher explained that her class experts are the children who have computers at home and:

> They highlight things and get the idea that you can move it. It's like anything if you use it often you get confident. If something goes wrong they say 'Oh you do this, this and this', sometimes they're right.

She described one student she was talking to about his poor handwriting who told her that he did not have to learn to write because when he goes to work *'we'll be using computers'*.

Both these projects were successful because the teachers had carefully thought about the structures for the pieces in advance (even if they did change from the original idea) and because there was additional support in the classroom. Although the structure was entirely teacher led, the storylines were student created and this gave the students a real sense of it being 'theirs'. This is reinforced by students this age using themselves as characters in their stories, so that the story is not only their schoolwork, but they are out rescuing someone in a submarine or flying off to Saturn. Both projects were concerned with analysing story structure, and to that end both class teachers felt that the students had gained in the process. Technically, students were becoming more skilled and were building confidence with using the computer, but arguably more importantly, they were also beginning to develop concepts about the nature of computers and what it is possible to do with multimedia authoring. With the necessary support, learning in this context can be extended, however without this it may be difficult to focus on the relevant aspects, and they may not achieve these goals. This does make multimedia authoring with 5–7 year olds more teacher intensive than a similar project with older students, but they seem to make useful gains and the teachers involved in these projects were all keen to continue with further multimedia authoring work.

Chapter 14

Special needs in primary schools

This chapter describes two multimedia authoring projects in primary schools involving groups of students statemented as having special educational needs (SEN). A statement of SEN is the outcome of a process that identifies and assesses the specific needs of individual students with SEN. The statement details the statutory requirements for that student, any specific needs, educational objectives, and additional support needed from outside the school. This could range from a small amount of classroom help from a learning support assistant within a mainstream primary school, to full time special school provision. In these two case studies the students statemented for SEN received additional help from specialist support teachers from the Hackney Primary and Specialist Support Team. These special needs teachers come into the school for a period of time each week to support the students' learning and to help these students integrate into mainstream primary schools. The teachers work with the students both in the classroom and on a withdrawal basis.

Statemented students were chosen as the focus of these two projects for a number of reasons. First, these students are often singled out and withdrawn from the classroom for extra curriculum support, but are rarely given the 'high status' and 'fun' ways of working. For students who often have low self-esteem, how they are seen by their classmates is very important. It was hoped that the rest of the class would appreciate that these students were learning exciting new skills that they would like to learn too, and that this might encourage them to see the students with SEN as people with something to offer. Second, although students with SEN often have a short attention span, the computers as an outside focus can increase their levels of concentration, resulting in more substantial achievements with something to show for their efforts. Finally, the nature of making multimedia, as seen, requires an audience. The immediate audience of classmates could provide important positive feedback to the students with SEN, giving them a greater sense of success and satisfaction than is their usual classroom experience.

Both projects described, *Animals in action* and *Pollution* came from curriculum science work. The projects, although similar, bring out different aspects of the process. *Animals in action* focuses on the nature of the subject learning through the multimedia work. It is a description of what happened in the classroom. *Pollution* gives a sense of the increase in self-esteem and motivation experienced by the students involved in the project. Both these pieces are presented in full on the CD ROM.

Example 1: *Animals in action*

Project focus: Animals in their habitats
Curriculum area: Science
Age group: Year 5/6 (9–11 year olds)
Group structure: A group of six students, three statemented for SEN
Location: Three computers at the side of the classroom
Time: One morning a week for 7 weeks

(This example is based on Lachs (1999).)

This project consisted of a mixed ability group where three of the students had SEN statements for language and learning and behavioural difficulties. Three teachers were involved in supporting the project – the class teacher and two SEN support teachers. The project ran for one morning a week for 7 weeks with two teachers working with the group at any one time. Three computers were set up in the classroom, so the project work went on alongside regular classwork. The class teacher moved between working with the whole class and the computer group, the support teachers were each there for half a morning, just working with the computer group. I was there initially to teach the skills, and then to act as technical backup. The students were put into pairs, with a statemented student in each pair. As one of the support teachers explained:

> One child with specific learning difficulties had amazing insight and knowledge and aural capacity, but was lost when it came to the writing. It was important that he was paired with a child confident with writing.

The science being studied was animals in their habitats. The structure for the project was decided by the teachers who chose three habitats for the students to look at: a desert, a rainforest and the Hackney Marshes. The rest of the structure, research, design and presentation was left to the students. Each pair took one of the habitats, located it (there are lots of deserts and rainforests in the world) and found three animals that live there. They had to be specific. Rather than choose a generic monkey, they had to find out that, for example, the black spider monkey lived in the area of rainforest they had located in South America. Having done this, they looked at what homes the animals have, what they eat and how they move. They found information from library books as the school did not have any relevant CD ROMs and was not connected to the Internet. A title screen for the *Animals in action* project is shown in Screen shot 14.1

Initially the students wrote out their questions and answers on large sheets of paper, aware that each question and answer would be on one screen, but not designing the screens in any detail. They assumed a linear format where each animal had between three and five screens running in sequence one to the next. This basic structure remained the same, but ideas were changed and added to as more information was learned and researched during the project. This meant that students were finding out the information off the computer and then presenting it on the computer.

The animals were all drawn straight on to the computer by the students using the mouse, and without using clipart from elsewhere. This was crucial to their

Screen shot 14.1 Title screen with menu choices.

understanding of animal movement and behaviour as they had to know the details in order to be able to draw them correctly. The discussion around how things should look improved the quality and the accuracy of the drawings. In drawing the Toco Toucan, for example, the students realised that they did not know how many claws a toucan had. They found out from a book that it has three claws, but were then left discussing how a toucan would sit on a branch. As one of the teachers explained:

> *You can learn a piece of information from a book, but it then needs putting into practice. It's like reading a recipe is different to doing it in practice, trying it out, finding out how it works. By actually drawing the toucan they could see that there was no way it could have three claws on the front of the branch. It would keel over forward . . . It was very rewarding to see SEN children producing text and drawings that were far above any expectations before this project.*

The toucan that was drawn is shown in Screen shot 14.2.

Paired designing, drawing and animating made it essential for the students to talk to each other. It was clear that different students had different skills, and that it was very beneficial to pair a student with English as a second language with a student with English as a first language, and a student with literacy difficulties with a more fluent reader. It had other spin-offs, as one of the teachers described: *'The collaborative aspect was invaluable not only for sharing knowledge, but for building self-esteem'*.

Apart from vague ideas from pets or wildlife television, the students had no direct experience to help them think about how animals move. Their teacher suggested that they explored moving themselves with specific constraints. In the school hall they experimented with different possibilities: using two legs (like a grey heron on Hackney Marshes), or four legs (like a camel in the desert), or with four legs but your whole body along the ground (like a gecko in the desert) (see Screen shot 14.3). When they had an idea of what might work, they checked pictures and text, although they did not have access to video. One of the SEN teachers stressed: *'They were discovering by doing it, finding which legs moved when and then animating it crystallises it* [the information]'.

Screen shot 14.2 Toucan sitting on a branch.

Screen shot 14.3 Experimenting with four legs.

Before they began animating, the students sketched what would be on each screen so that they could be sure of getting the sequence correct. This was very effective, as a support teacher explained:

> *The animation was so motivating. Putting in the stages in order for it to move. It's a breakthrough in ordering the sequencing of the animation. They understand the movement and relating it to cartoons on the telly. Special Educational Needs students need concrete examples and apparatus. The animation brings it to life in a concrete way.*

One of the students with very poor concentration found herself working on her own one week as her partner was absent. She spent the whole morning animating a spider spinning a web (Screen shot 14.4). It was time consuming, but the benefits for her were very apparent to her support teacher who said:

The child with severe special educational needs loved it because she could do it. She remembered very clearly how to do it and was able to help a child who missed a session.

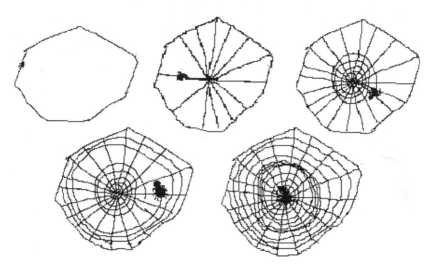

Screen shot 14.4 Sequence of animation for a spider spinning a web.

The possibilities of using multiple media meant that the students could find different ways of showing information. The animation did not explain everything, so text and sound were added to complete the picture. The choice of what medium to use for what piece of information was the students' decision. The pair working on the rainforest had animated the toucan picking up a berry when they found out that it had a tongue. After much discussion they decided to re-do the animation, adding the toucan opening and closing its mouth before it picked up the berry in order to show its tongue. They spoke an explanatory voice-over: *'The toucan has a very thin long tongue to help it move food around its mouth'*. They had been very excited at finding this information and creative in how they presented it.

The students became very engaged in the project, surprising all involved with their level of concentration. *'They had extraordinary patience'*, said one of the teachers, *'They didn't seem to mind if they lost a page, they were just motivated to move on'*. The quality of the piece they produced shows this motivation, it is very careful, interesting and humorous.

Example 2: *Pollution*

Project focus: Pollution
Curriculum area: Science
Age group: Year 4 (8–9 year olds)
Group structure: A group of six students all statemented for SEN
Location: Three computers in an open area just outside the classroom
Time: One morning a week for 7 weeks

This project involved a group of six students all statemented for SEN. Their class teacher described them as having *'emotional, social and academic'* needs. They had regular support from an SEN teacher from the Hackney Primary and Specialist Support Team both within the classroom and withdrawn for special intensive curriculum support. The students had low self-esteem, low ability and low concentration, finding it very difficult to work without constant encouragement and help. Their support teacher describes them as children who: *'can't hold information, can't sequence, forget what they're doing, forget the task'.*

Pollution was the class science topic which was being taught by their teacher in the classroom to the whole class. The multimedia project was being taught by the support teacher and myself in the open-plan library just outside the classroom. The computers were not used regularly in the class, so this project was seen as something special. The class teacher was particularly keen on all of her special needs students doing this project because they rarely had a high status and positive learning experience as a special piece of work different from the rest of the class. In fact other class members were so curious about the project, they often found excuses to leave the classroom and have a look at what the computer group were doing.

The support teacher had used multimedia authoring before with SEN students and was very enthusiastic about working in this way. She said that part of her pleasure was in the fact that the students *'didn't have to get pencils and the pencils didn't break, and all the things that usually delayed them didn't happen'* because the *'screen contained them'.* The screen indeed contained the pens and pencils that were needed for the drawing as well as providing an outside focus for their attention. However, they still needed a lot of support to get the project going. Although it was more teacher intensive than a non-computer project, these six students needed additional support most of the time even within the regular classroom.

The process the students went through was similar to the *Animals in action* project. Over seven afternoons the students researched, planned, designed and authored pictures drawn straight on to the computer, text, sound and animation. The students worked in pairs at three computers which were moved into the library specifically for the project, so students did not have a chance to continue this work in the rest of the week. They began with planning off the computer, brainstorming ideas on a piece of paper. This was unfamiliar to them and they found it very difficult, partly because they were squabbling over who would sit where and who would do the writing and partly because they were so excited about the prospect of doing a special computer project that they were already arguing about who would do the first drawing on the screen.

Although they found planning hard, the process stuck in their minds. During a discussion with these students almost a year after the project was completed, when they were asked if they remembered how they planned it, one of the boys answered:

> *We planned on paper, put a word in the middle and drew a circle around it, and drew lines and at the end of them wrote something. First Miss showed us then we done it by ourselves.*

Although he could not remember what those words were, he did remember what he did. Indeed the support teacher described a piece of classwork some time after the project ended where the teacher asked the class to make a storyboard, and these students found it easy to do. As special needs students often find processes difficult, this was very useful.

Most of the project time was taken up with drawing. The difficulty with controlling the mouse to draw straight on to the computer was frustrating for the students as two of them discussed. One student commented, *'the pencil [tool on the screen] was hard and wobbly'*, and the second added, *'you can't keep your balance on the [screen] pencil or paintbrush. You need to keep rubbing out bits'*. Despite these difficulties the students persisted. When asked if it was easier to draw off the computer, although wavering they would not say yes. This may have been because they wanted to work on the computer and felt that agreeing with this statement would mean less computer time. It seems that although it was tricky to draw on the computer, they enjoyed it.

The support teacher described her own tension and frustration that the students might lose their work easily because: *'they wanted to press every button available'*. However as the project progressed she described that:

> *no one freaked out about making mistakes and they ended up with a piece of work. They learned they could make a mistake and then mend it again and not lose everything, and they can't do that with writing on paper when they see that their writing looks untidy and a page is full of mistakes. The computer is never a page of mistakes. It's neat and tidy and has order to it.*

During this process the students' concentration increased and as their concentration developed, their arguments began to lessen.

Most of their drawings were part of making animations. One animation showed a ship leaking oil into the sea and a fish being covered with the oil and dying. Another animation had a girl spraying her hair with an aerosol, the gas from the spray rising and going through the ozone layer making a hole, the sunlight's ultra violet rays then coming down through the hole, and someone lying on a beach getting burned. Both animations were complex and involved the students drawing a range of screens which were then linked together to create a moving animation. As one student described it:

> *to move the man's arm, we had to draw one part and then rub out the arm and draw another arm and, then draw another arm, and when you look at it, it don't look like you had to rub it out 'cos it's all the same.*

Although this description leaves a lot unsaid for the listener to fill in the gaps, for this student it is a good explanation of the order of making an animation. Two pictures from an animation on pollution from smoking are shown in Screen shot 14.5.

Screen shot 14.5 Part of an animation on pollution from smoking.

The support teacher felt that one reason for their improved concentration was that they really associated with the pictures they were drawing and the ideas they were espousing because:

> It's living. When you see the boat moving, L and F were driving that boat. It's all real. You'd get the same thing if you could do drama with them You're living what's going on . . . the animation made it come alive, one minute you're one place, next the next. It's cause and effect and these children don't understand it. Where do they see the process of pollution and its effects? But there on the computer, they could see it.

One image of a ship causing pollution by leaking oil is shown in Screen shot 14.6.

Putting their own voices on to the computer was the feature that the students unanimously voted as their favourite part. These students generally found it hard to describe ideas and talk about their work. In class they would not often be chosen to speak, and they would not volunteer. Their support teacher likened recording their voices to the students seeing themselves as presenters on television. This would be both familiar and motivating to students who: 'have such low self-esteem and don't have the vocabulary to talk about things'. She went on to describe how the next year, the class was doing some work with a tape recorder, and whereas otherwise they may well have sat and giggled rather than being able to record their voices, they were less afraid of it and could just get on with it.

The students' self-esteem was certainly increased. One girl made a humorous but rather gruesome animation of a woman taking her dog for a walk, the dog defecating and walking off and then a baby crawling up and eating the faeces. The support teacher explained that: 'usually the class are laughing at her, but here they were laughing with her. It made her feel very proud'. The class teacher, although not involved in the project, did see the results in the students' classroom work and was very positive about the

This ship is pouring oil into the water because it is leaking. It is polluting the water.

Click on the ship.

Screen shot 14.6 Beginning of an animation of a ship dropping oil into the sea.

change in their self-esteem. She wrote in evaluation of the project: *'the project instilled something within the children, that shadowed, with confidence, their work in other areas of learning'*.

Certainly the students' excitement affected their ability to learn. The pair working on air pollution found out information about CFCs. They spent a long time muttering and repeating 'chlorofluorocarbon' under their breath while they were working. The following week when I entered the school, the two boys came charging towards me and the first one, catching his breath, said excitedly: 'Chlorofluorocarbon'. When working with SEN students steps may be small, but they are important. Whether or not they remembered what CFCs had to do with pollution and whether or not they would remember it long term, these two students had been motivated enough to hold this information in their heads for the whole week. The students did not learn massive amounts of information, the project was more important in terms of their gains in confidence and self-esteem, and as the support teacher described, it was different to *'reading the books and writing it out'*.

On the negative side there were some issues that could have worked better. The support teacher felt that there could have been more planning with the school as a whole. Although these students benefited, if they had been in mixed ability groupings, other members of the class would have been there to witness their achievements. As it was, at the end of the pollution project the whole class ran an assembly. Those students who had been doing work in the classroom could hold pictures up, but it was more difficult to show the computer work: *'The school would have been bowled over to see it, but they needed a big screen. This is really a management issue'*, their support teacher said.

After the project was over one of the students who is very timid and quiet was so enamoured with computers that his parents saved up and bought one. When I was back in the school a year later and asked the students questions about the project he did not take any part in the discussion. However when I asked him directly how he felt about his new computer at home he became bright eyed and articulate and said:

> *It was fun 'cos I knew what it was and how to use everything. They are fun 'cos you could do all different things – play games, speak instead of typing it out, drawing, writing, playing cards and going on the Internet.*

The project had given him a new interest that he had continued to develop.

The project in whatever limited way was a success, maybe not in terms of learning specific factual information but in terms of emotional gains. Leaving the last words to the class teacher who knew the students best, she felt that the project brought the students: *'to a clear focus where happiness in succeeding overcame their barriers'* and that their new confidence *'helped them rise to the challenge of new learning situations which might otherwise have seemed scary to them'*.

From both these projects it is clear that the special needs students gained significantly from this experience, and some of it has stayed with them. First, they achieved something academically, which is not an everyday feature of their school lives, and had a tangible product to show for it that could be viewed by their peers. Second, because they were given this opportunity to achieve and to be seen to do so, it left them feeling very proud of themselves and increased their self-esteem. The major issue and difficulty however is one of resources. These projects were possible and successful because there was additional staffing from support teachers. A whole class multimedia authoring project in a classroom or a computer room can be managed with one teacher, however a small group of special needs students require more individual attention.

Chapter 15

Teachers' experience

This chapter is based on interviews with three teachers talking about using multimedia authoring with students. They described how it affected their teaching styles and explained how their ideas, confidence and competence developed as they continued to use multimedia authoring with different classes or in different areas of the curriculum.

Tracy is the ICT co-ordinator and deputy head of a one form entry primary school located in the middle of a working class Hackney estate. The students in the school, mostly from the estate, are from a number of different cultural backgrounds and speak many different languages. There is one computer in every classroom; in Tracy's room it is next to a carpeted area where the students sit together, so it is well placed for whole class teaching. Before using multimedia authoring with her class, Tracy was confident with using word processing and a few pieces of educational subject-specific software with her class but wanted to move herself and the staff forward. A multimedia authoring project was begun involving an artist/IT consultant who came in for four initial sessions to help plan and get the project under way, in this case the *Tudor maze* – based on the Tudors in history. At an initial meeting the teacher, the IT consultant and myself discussed how to create a general structure for the piece as a whole. The decision was to use a maze as a central focus for information screens to link to, where students would create screens depicting the maze and aspects of Tudor life (this project has been referred to in Chapters 1 and 7 and can be seen in full on the CD ROM). Tracy spoke of her inability in that first meeting to grasp basic concepts of multimedia as she had not seen other students' multimedia work at that point and relied on the consultant who seemed to know what he was talking about. She explained that she had no real notion of how a multimedia authoring project could work in a classroom, both in terms of what skills the students would need to acquire and in terms of classroom organisation: '*I had no idea at all. As we were talking about the maze I couldn't actually envisage it. From that point onwards, it was a whole learning process for me*'. However, as the computer was already incorporated into classroom practice, multimedia authoring was not difficult to integrate as Tracy acknowledged that she simply adapted her standard way of teaching to the process of multimedia authoring.

After looking at other students' multimedia authoring work and seeing how different screens would link together, Tracy described her growing confidence:

> *straight away I had more of an idea, of different ways of visualising things. In terms of being able to teach it, within two weeks I knew quite a lot . . . It had its own momentum – to learn one thing, you had to learn another – and it was*

interesting, a new way of approaching an old thing and when you've been teaching for ten years any new approach is accepted with gratitude.

As she was discovering new things, so were the students and this seemed like a good way of keeping the exploration going.

They asked, 'Is it possible to . . .?' or 'can we . . .?' Their questioning led us to investigate further. If I'd just have gone on a course it wouldn't have had the same impact. It lent a purpose and urgency to it. If 29 ten year olds are going 'so what if . . .?' you can't say 'I don't know', you've got to say 'let's try'.

Naomi is the deputy head in a one form entry junior school. There is a small computer room with six to eight computers (depending on how many are working at any time), a scanner and tables in the centre. The room is too small for a whole class to work there comfortably, so either they do and it is very crowded, or the class is split which then requires an extra teacher to work with the other half of the class. Naomi was tentative but enthusiastic about using ICT, and keen to start using multimedia authoring as she had seen a project of multimedia animations in science that a fellow teacher had completed the previous term. Naomi began her first project, which was also initially supported by an artist/IT consultant, with some understanding of the general concept and structure of multimedia, but like Tracy, she had no idea how it would practically work in the classroom. Her project was *Greek myths and legends*, which she used as a basis for finding out information on the Ancient Greeks. She commented:

I knew what I wanted to do with the stories and to teach through the stories but actually what it all consisted of, I didn't know how the artwork and the computer would work together.

Frank is a science teacher in a secondary school round the corner from Naomi's junior school. He is an advocate of using computers in the classroom and tries to integrate them into his science teaching as much as possible. Before using multimedia authoring he had used *Powerpoint* with students to create small slide show presentations, desktop publishing to make multimedia posters, and was involved in getting the school connected to the Internet. He was particularly interested in finding ways into science that were creative enough to draw in those students who may otherwise be turned off the subject. He explained:

we don't have a great degree of control about what we teach, but we can control how we teach it. We subject specialists tend to present it in an academic way which only hits about 10% of our pupils. If you dress up the subject, you get a completely different subject.

The school has two computer rooms and one computer that can be taken into the science lab. For whole class teaching, logistical somersaults need to be performed to find times that the computer room is free that coincide with the lesson time required, or making a deal with the IT teacher to swap rooms for a week or two.

Structure of the multimedia projects

Both the primary school teachers' first multimedia authoring projects had linear structures with branches. Tracy's *Tudor maze* was a series of sequential screens (the maze) with offshoots (dead-ends and screens of Tudor information). Although this structure had been planned by the teacher before the project began, the detailed planning of which screen linked to which and what information would be added was left to the students. Naomi's *Greek myths and legends* project was a series of stories, each consisting of five or six screens. At some point in each story there was a link to a screen containing information about a particular aspect of Greek life. The structure was therefore simple and did not need planning, however students sketched designs of screens so that they could split the story into chunks.

By the time Tracy and Naomi were planning their next multimedia authoring projects, they were both critical of the linearity of their first projects, moving on to creating more complex structures with students. Tracy maintained that she:

> *didn't explore the full potential of multimedia. I was still approaching it like it was pencil and paper, each separate card [screen] was a thing in itself and then you just put them all together at the end, so it was more like a gallery than an interactive media.*

She described how both she and a new class of students the following year, having seen and used the *Tudor maze* were coming up with different ideas. This class, also studying the Tudors, had to find a different way of approaching it. Although it was these students' first project, they were starting from a point of familiarity with presentations, having critically analysed the work of students they knew. As Tracy's experience developed, her expectations of what the students could do with multimedia authoring were higher. Tracy compared her development to *'building blocks'* and this is clear by the more complex hierarchical structure of the second Tudor project.

Naomi felt her Ancient Greece project was as much about getting used to the medium as presenting curriculum work, and a second project on climate in geography was much more developed than the first. She described the difference in the structures of the two projects. In the first piece:

> *all it was was a story and it went through the story and from each page it would go off to another page. The Arachne story was teaching about clothes and on one page there'd be something about the clothes of the time, but it always came back to the story. Just one page off and then back to the story again. This one [her second project] this year goes all over the place.*

Frank's first multimedia authoring project was *Genetic engineering and selective breeding*, with a very lively year 9 (13–14 year olds) class (see Chapter three, example 2). This project was only partially successful as the students found the task difficult. Frank had split the material into manageable chunks but left the students to plan out a map for their specific area. Although they had been shown other student work and the non-linear nature of multimedia was discussed, most students only cursorily planned their pieces, finishing off for homework. This meant that some students planned badly, lost their plans or did not plan at all. The outcome of these situations was essentially linear pieces. Frank felt that he himself had not been sufficiently prepared, and that he only really knew the importance of the planning stage after the project was well under way. He would have liked each group or pair to have information packs so that they could have been clearer about the information they were to present. He felt that this first project did not have enough structure to contain the students. Frank's next project, with a different class, was much more limited. He set out a series of linked screens ready-made for the students and told them what to do on each screen. The first had a specific theme where they drew a poster off the computer and scanned it in as a background. Frank explained this way of working: *'There's flexibility, but there are three blank cards with text boxes, and they just type in and import backgrounds, otherwise there's too much to learn at the same time'*. Frank felt that pre-made screens could introduce students to concepts at a more manageable rate.

Although the teachers were critical of their initial forays into multimedia authoring, they were successful in that the students were engaged and learned from the process and produced, for the most part, quality work. Working on a linear project before moving towards something more complex and interactive seemed to be a useful first step in the primary school teachers' understanding of multimedia and of how to teach it. In advocating 'learning by doing' for students it is important to remember that teachers can develop new classroom strategies in a similar way and first projects can give teachers the ideas, confidence and enthusiasm to continue to use multimedia authoring in the curriculum. As these teachers became more confident with the possibilities of the medium, they felt more able to encourage students in new and creative areas of learning.

Multimedia elements

The maze screens of the *Tudor maze* were simply pictures and animations without text. The information screens were mainly text with an illustrative picture. *Greek myths and legends* also used text as the main medium and although the artwork was very beautiful, it was like a picture book, as an accompaniment to the text. By the second projects both teachers used images as a way in, and these images suggested interactive possibilities, sound and text to the students. Tracy described her movement from encouraging the students to start with the written ideas and adding images, to starting with the images. In her second project some screens had no written text at all, using sound instead of writing. The school had bought a scanner and digital camera and the students were becoming familiar with how to use them. The scanner opened new ways of thinking for Tracy and her students. Tracy described how it produced greater integration with other work going on in the classroom, because whatever artwork the students now produced in other contexts, they wanted to scan it into multimedia computer projects.

Naomi's school had a scanner in the computer room from before her first multimedia authoring project. The students had scanned in paintings, pencil sketches, wax etching and collage for the Greek myths, each story using a different medium. The artwork was fabulous, however it took until a second project on climate to really begin to use the artwork as a way of conveying information rather than being simply illustrative.

Frank described the students' balance between 'artwork' and 'content'. He saw the content as contained in text and that drawings were useful as illustrations. He described how students would at times *'get lost in drawing and forget content'*. He explained the mixture of abilities and outlook of the class: '*Some recognise content as the critical thing, others just want to do nice pictures and they then see someone doing animation and want to do that. They may have an overview but lose sight of it*'. It certainly brought into clear relief the conviction that next time he would give students a much more detailed and specific task rather than let them make too many choices. He also used a scanner as an essential part of the kit, but pointed out that it does give the teacher another thing to learn:

> *You need to know how to scan and appreciate what it looks like when scanned. You need to be confident from an IT point of view, you don't need to know everything, but need confidence to work out a way of doing things.*

Creativity in the classroom

Both primary students and teachers had become more confident with special effects such as animation, pop-up text boxes and making dragable items, and this meant that the students' ideas around interactivity were expanded, although they then wanted to drag everything: flags on to capital cities, clothes on to characters, weather symbols on to maps, quotations from plays on to the character that said them or parts of a flower into the right place. Once students had seen what was possible, they used it to abundance. It is interesting to ask the question, when students know the software, do they stop coming out with ideas that cannot be done, in favour of things they know they can do? And do they then choose to overuse certain aspects because they know how to use them?

Frank's enthusiasm about multimedia authoring was about finding ways to incorporate creativity into the science curriculum. He is concerned with the students who are not succeeding in science and particularly wants them to achieve something and not be left with failure. He considers that students should be able to contribute to science lessons in any way they can, and if this is through art or role play then that is still a contribution:

> *We need more rounded lessons and let kids show what they can do – to present science work in a more creative way if not scientific. Science is a creative act but kids don't do that. It's difficult to be creative in science but they could be creative in a scientific context. Multimedia allows a high element of creative working, artistic or linguistic. Dressing science up with multimedia can force them to reformulate ideas, and learning is about reformulating ideas.*

Future use of multimedia authoring

Tracy's next multimedia project was about rainforests. This was with a class who were by now familiar with multimedia authoring and produced work that was more sophisticated, in that students were encouraged to put a stronger focus on audience and to try the project out with a representative sample as they went along. Tracy explained how she made a point of discussing this issue on an ongoing basis in feedback time at the end of each session. This focus meant that interactive elements were more carefully thought out, so that instead of dragging or animating just because they could, students were more concerned with using these aspects to put their point across as clearly as possible. Looking forwards, Tracy wants to extend the use of multimedia authoring in the school to all teachers, encouraging greater collaboration between classes, so that each class can be working on a part of a larger school project.

Naomi continued working with her class on a project to include animation. She began with the class making animations off the computer as a prelude to producing animated presentations of poems, with interactive games to accompany them.

Frank wants to start multimedia authoring earlier on in the school, using pre-made screens that teach students to link screens together before starting completely from scratch. He is also interested in how useful it could be for students with special needs. He described a 14-year-old boy who was an *absolute terror, impossibly difficult, attention seeking and couldn't string three words together or cope with year 9 work'*. He decided that he would give him an individual multimedia authoring project where he was asked to tell a story about ways that you can keep things warm. He described that after a few weeks the boy was really skilled at using the software, and delighted to show the class how to make buttons and link screens. *'From a real pain'*, Frank admitted *'he was as quiet as ever in front of the computer'*.

Teachers' approach

The most significant development for the teachers was the increased amount of class discussion and criticism that evolved. All the teachers felt that as they became more confident with what multimedia authoring could do, they became more able to discuss issues of audience, interactivity and design with the students. This gave them the space to concentrate on the quality of the work, which affected the structure of the classes, using opening and feedback sessions to explore ideas and respond to criticism. It also affected the quality of the artwork for scanning and interactivity. Tracy explained that knowing the possibilities and gathering new ideas had opened up countless new options. Frank insisted on the importance of taking one step back and being critical of what you were doing.

Advice to other teachers

Tracy, as ICT co-ordinator is concerned with encouraging the use of multimedia authoring across the school and across the curriculum. She is eager for other teachers to take it up, as they are doing slowly. Tracy specifies that: *'this term multimedia does actually mean multi in its true sense that you can use it in many different ways'*. Naomi feels confident enough to run staff meetings on the technical skills needed, but she cautions that you forget things quickly when you are not using them, and running a second project was vital for remembering how to do it. She also is aware that her project was pretty extensive and that teachers can work with their class on: *'just linking one card to another with a button. It doesn't have to be a big elaborate project'*. Frank's advice to other teachers is similar, to start with something simple, possibly using pre-made screens, and once the students have grasped that concept it is not a big jump to creating their own presentations from scratch.

Chapter 16

Choosing software and resources

There is a wide selection of multimedia and web authoring software to choose from and it ranges from simple children's programs that are contained and prescriptive, to complex industry standard programs that are extremely versatile, but may require a knowledge of programming. Progression, as in all areas of education is an important consideration in choosing software. This will either result in using different software for different ages and abilities, or finding a piece of software that has progression built in through the ability to access the program on different levels. If progression is built in, students will be able to use the same program to create simple linear stories as well as more complex non-linear designs, so allowing them to develop with the software as they get older. This will particularly assist mixed ability groupings, including students with special needs, all using the same software.

The basic requirements programs must have in order to be called multimedia or web authoring programs are that they allow screens of multimedia holding text, sound, images, animation and video to be linked together in various ways. There will then be additional features that need consideration, including the current differences between multimedia authoring and web authoring.

The overlap between multimedia and web authoring software is large, however the technology is not identical. The purpose of multimedia authoring software is for people to make their own presentations and software. It is essentially image based using full screen graphics, animations and video, and can include sophisticated interactivity. This needs to run up to speed and can be stored on the computer itself or on a CD ROM. There are currently many products on the market that are aimed at young people and have built in progression for multimedia authoring. The purpose of web authoring is to share information with a wide audience and get feedback. Websites offer extended possibilities for linking, not only within the website, but out into the wider Internet as well, enabling two-way communication. Although theoretically everything that can be done in multimedia authoring can be done on the web, web communications technology is (as I write) still too slow for full screen animation, lengthy sounds and video, and still too difficult for students to make some of the more complex interactive features. Students are therefore restricted to a more text-based medium using smaller images and animations in a more illustrative way. However it is important to be aware that the direction is towards all multimedia being 'on-line'. As web technology advances, wider bandwidth gives quicker connections and web authoring software for students becomes more similar to multimedia authoring software; eventually these two technologies may merge. Indeed, some web authoring packages already on the market allow the user to embed multimedia presentations within a website. The combination of fully interactive, full screen multimedia which is easy to make, in association with all the possibilities for communication that the web offers is a very attractive future development. For now, a decision on the most sensible software to choose should be based on what you are going to do with it. Therefore, for making interactive curriculum presentations and games, use multimedia authoring software, and for making websites for wide exposure and the possibility of feedback, use web authoring software.

Structure of software

There are two types of authoring programs. Some programs are integrated, which means they contain all the elements that are needed to produce a presentation – that is, the ability to paint, write, animate and add sound and video all within the same program. These would also offer the option of importing images from scanners, digital cameras or other programs. The second type of multimedia authoring program is more like an authoring shell. It offers a framework for drawing together the media into an interactive environment, but the different media would have to be created separately in painting programs, animation programs, sound files and word processors and then imported into the authoring program.

The most common conceptualisation for a multimedia authoring program is the idea of linking individual screens together by using buttons, hot spots or hypertext links. However there are programs that use a completely different way of thinking about multimedia authoring, such as the concept of a film score which is constantly moving and animating, where the author needs to stop the movement in order to get static images. Although the software can produce similar presentations, the concepts and ways of using them are very different.

In all authoring software there are a number of things that should be taken into consideration.

Progression

As multimedia authoring projects in schools are well suited to progression educationally in terms of development from simple illustrated stories to complex interactive presentations, the software must reflect this. In primary schools the software needs to be user-friendly enough for young children to draw and write relatively unaided. If this is not possible to do within the package itself, there needs to be a simple import feature for them to collate their piece. It is important that the progression is not simply about drawing or writing, but about the way the media are combined and linked together. Towards the end of primary school age the software will need to include many more sophisticated features, including adding buttons that have a variety of presentation and interactive features. At secondary level the software should be able to be more tailored by the students to suit their own needs.

Interface

Interface means what the program looks like on the screen. The interface should be pleasant to look at and a nice space to work in. If it is colourful, a good size to read and child-friendly looking, it can give students motivation and a sense of fun.

Ease of use

The program should be easy to learn, easy to use and easy to remember. If a program looks too complicated it will not provide an incentive to work out how to use it, and can become frustrating. There should be some consistency as to how features work, shortcuts are always useful and being able to backtrack easily through previous screens is important.

Interactive capabilities

The program must be able to support features that allow student authors to make their presentation interactive for their audience. The basic interactivity students create will be the linking of screens together with buttons or hypertext so that the audience can navigate through the piece. However, interactivity is not just about the audience being able to choose which buttons to click on to move to other screens, it is also about the audience having 'things to do' in order to 'play the game'. The author must therefore be able to create different interactive elements by making buttons or hot spots that will enable the audience to:

- move objects around the screen
- answer a question by typing on the screen or clicking yes/no buttons
- control when to see animations or video.

The interactive elements need to give the author control over how the piece looks and the user control over how they view the presentation, and it needs to be accessible without complex programming. This tends to be more available on multimedia authoring than web authoring programs.

Showing the links

It is very useful if the program can create a diagrammatic representation of the piece as it is being worked on, showing the screens and links. In these types of diagrams it should also be possible to drag and move screens to change their position in the design, and to break and remake links.

Presentation features

It is important that students can make the screen look as they want it to. For the web, one piece of software will be the authoring program, but another will be the viewing program. The students need to be able to have a sense of what the piece will really look like.

Graphics

Graphics are usually the most ubiquitous medium in multimedia authoring. The program needs to be able to:

- use a variety of colours and textures
- have a variety of tools

- be able to transform images, rotate, reflect and re-size them
- import images from other programs, scanners and digital cameras.

In web authoring, images will need to be imported from another program. This is easiest if the author can drag and drop images on to the screen where they would like them to be. It is also useful if authoring software has a selection of ready-made clipart and animations, and possibly patterns and textures.

Animation

There are three types of animation. The first is where the image on the screen moves along a path but does not change in itself, for example a ball bouncing. This is useful for making things look fun, flashy and humorous and is often used to good effect in titles where words move across the screen. The second type of animation is where the image itself changes but it does not move along a path, like a seed growing, where many images slightly altered are drawn and each separate image is flicked through as in a flick book. Finally there can be a combination of the two, with the image both changing and moving along a specified path; for example, a runner running, where there may be several images of the runner as well as movement across the screen. Check that all these options are possible. For multimedia authoring programs large animations should be possible, for web authoring they will be smaller.

Text

When using text in multimedia authoring be aware that whatever font you use will need to be on other computers, otherwise the computer will choose the nearest approximation. It is more sensible to use system and popular fonts. For web authoring the choice of fonts will be limited by the software.

Sound

Sound needs to be easy to record. Multimedia computers come with sound cards. Some computers have built in microphones and speakers, others will need to have them added. The software itself needs to support sound. Integrated programs should have a built-in recording feature. They may save sounds embedded in the presentation, or save them in a separate file connected to the presentation. Programs should be able to import sounds.

Layers

There may be a number of layers on the screen. Text may be on one layer, graphics on another, and so on. There needs to be a simple way of moving between the layers and relayering with ease.

Programming

Multimedia and web authoring programs tend to use templates which allow the user to do many things without ever touching a programming language. This is fine for the vast majority of users, however doing what the program wants you to do can leave you with presentations that look much the same as everyone else's. For greater independence of identity and sophistication a programming language will have to be learned. On the web the basic programming languages are Hypertext Markup Language (HTML) and JAVA. In multimedia authoring programs, each program will use its own language. These are often complex languages which may on occasion be suitable for IT instruction or maths work, but may not be suitable for cross-curricular classroom work.

Documentation

Few students or teachers like trawling through computer manuals to find out how the software works, but good manuals can be extremely helpful. Some manuals do not come in paper form but are provided as on-line help or in a computerised help section of the program. Both electronic and paper manuals need to be simple enough for older students to use, with graphics and explanations. The most useful educational manuals I have seen incorporate ideas for how to use the program, and teachers' notes. If there are only electronic manuals and you find them difficult to use, you may need to order paper manuals. This documentation can be expensive.

Platform

Multimedia authoring software may be platform specific, that is, it only runs on a PC, Acorn or an Apple Macintosh or it may run across platforms. In schools or boroughs that have a mixture of machines it is important that the same software can be used on all machines. Web authoring software will not have this problem because the website will run from an Internet browser which will run on any platform. It is worth mentioning that different browsers display work slightly differently, so after making the piece, it is useful to check it on more than one browser before putting it up on the web.

Storing and sharing

Multimedia presentations can be stored on the computer they were made on, on a school intranet, on a zip disk or on a CD ROM. There may need to be a 'runtime version' or 'player' which will allow others to access the presentation. Although multimedia authoring programs are not designed for the web, they can be put on the web in two ways. Some programs have a 'plug-in' which is a piece of software that the web user can download in order to view the presentation. Alternatively, as mentioned before, some web authoring programs will allow you to embed the multimedia work within the website. In this way a more sophisticated multimedia presentation can be put inside a simpler web authoring program. This can be useful because rather than only seeing the multimedia presentation, it will be framed within the screen. This then gives the opportunity for a textual explanation of the context of the presentation. Multimedia pieces could be put into a school website; however, if this is the case, care will need to be taken over the size of the multimedia elements as the delivery speed will probably be slower. Web pages made by web authoring programs will be stored on your Internet provider's server and displayed as a website on the World Wide Web, which can then be accessed by anyone who has a connection to the Internet. Presentations for the web will need to be stored by you on your own computer, zip drive or CD ROM so that they can be changed and updated.

Software support

Most companies offer some software support, by phone line, e-mail or website.

Cost

Professional packages are expensive, especially if you need multiple copies for a computer room. Education packages tend to be more cost effective for schools, and companies may give good deals on bulk orders. Special licences that cover an entire LEA may also be available and offer competitive pricing. This approach encourages schools to share both information and ideas about using the software, and work that students have created.

Checklist for software

For any program, you need to find out what it can do and how easy it will be for the students to use. There may be a program that can do everything you want, but if it is really fiddly to use, it will not be touched. Students need to be able to have a go on their own and find things out for themselves. These questions need to be considered:

Is it an integrated program or a shell?
If it is an integrated program:

Can graphics be manipulated easily?
Is there good choice of colour and patterns?
Can it produce all three types of animation?
Is it easy to record sound?
Is the text processor easy to use, does it have a spell checker?

Can it make buttons of different sizes and shapes, both visible and invisible?
Are things easy to move around the screen (drag and drop)?
Does the working screen look nice, colourful, student-friendly?
Is it easy to move between the authoring screen and the display screen?
Is there progression built into the program?
Does it have ready-made buttons that have special effects such as moving text, hiding and showing objects?
Is it easy to create the interactivity for the user to move things around the screen?
Does it have a map showing the links?
Can this map be changed in order to alter the links?
Is it easy to make links?
Is it easy to change and edit features?
Is the program's programming language simple enough for students to use?
Is the documentation easy to read and/or access?
Will the program run on a variety of platforms?
Is there software support? What type?
Is it a reasonable price?

Tips for choosing software

- Talk to other teachers who have used the software.
- Talk to more than one software company.
- Read reviews in the Online section of the *Times Educational Supplement* and educational computing magazines.

Resources

There are some important resources that will make a multimedia or web authoring project much easier to integrate into classroom work. A scanner is probably an essential item, and a digital camera is very useful, and if using video, a video camera.

Scanners

These can be hand held or flat-bed. Hand held scanners are harder to control. Make sure the scanner comes with simple software. They are generally cheap and an expensive one is not needed.

Digital cameras

The market is flooded with digital cameras at different prices, some very cheap. A couple of tips: digital cameras need batteries and these can be used up quickly, so it may be useful to buy a power cable to use when transferring images from the camera to the computer. Also, some cameras display the image on a little monitor as you take the picture and if you switch this off it can save battery power. It is also important that the camera is robust and easy for students to use.

Video cameras

Your computer will need a video card with an extra socket for video input. You should be able to use any video camera. Digital video cameras are also available, but pricey.

Portable text processors

These are very convenient, especially in a one-computer classroom or where classes only have access to a computer room for a limited time each week. They need to be light and do not need any sophisticated features, just a basic word processor and a simple method of transfer to the computer.

CD writers

If you are saving multimedia presentations on to a CD ROM, you will need a CD writer to connect to your computer. This does not work in the same way as a floppy disk as you cannot overwrite previous files, just re-copy them on to the CD ROM. If you use a zip or a Jaz drive, they are simply like large floppy disks but will not fit into other computers unless they also have those drives.

Appendix 1: Design brief

This was a small project where a year-10 class (14 and 15 year olds) were working in pairs on a limited number of screens. (See Chapter 6, example 2.)

Genetically modified food

Multimedia genetics

Figure A1.1 Tins used in project on GM food.

The class is going to be working together on making a multimedia presentation about genetically modified food. This will be put on to a CD ROM with other pupils' work on genetics and will be given to other schools.

Imagine the tins in Figure A1.1 on a computer screen. Each one tin can be clicked on and it will move to another screen. Your pair is going to be working on one of these tins, which will mean making at least FOUR cards (screens).

Each card can have on it:

Pictures   These can be drawn, painted, made with collage, original photographs, and scanned on to the computer.

Text   Information is given in this pack. You may need to do more research or ask a teacher.

Sound   This can be voice-over explanations, sound effects, or reading the text in another language. It can be recorded directly on to the computer.

Animation   When you are familiar with the program, animation can be added if it is needed.

CARD 1:   A picture of the product and information about it.

CARD 2:   The argument for and against GM for this product *or* a relevant piece of information.

CARD 3:   The science behind GM or a relevant area.

CARD 4:   Two quiz questions that will check that people have read the information.

The first thing you need to do is plan out your cards on the back page. Turn to page 182 for an example.

On each card:

- sketch the image or describe the animation
- briefly outline the text in a few words
- briefly outline the sound in a few words.

Take into consideration:

- People don't read too much text. Some of it can be a voice-over.
- The text, sound and images should not repeat information but add to it.
- Write simply and clearly, the text needs to be understood by other people your age.
- Don't use ready-made images or copy text or there will be copyright issues.
- Don't use on-screen patterns or the piece will look like Hyperstudio, not your work.
- Make it interactive and fun so that you get your message across.

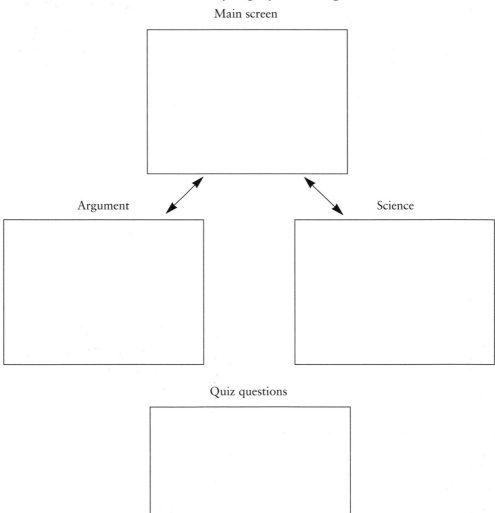

Appendix 2: Plans of student presentations

1. Alien from space

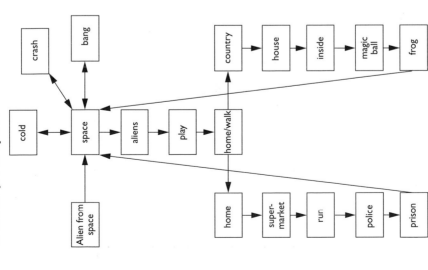

Figure A2.1 Plan for Alien from space.

2. The water cycle

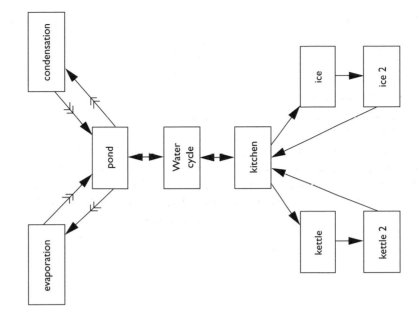

Figure A2.2 Plan for The water cycle.

3. Alive and not alive

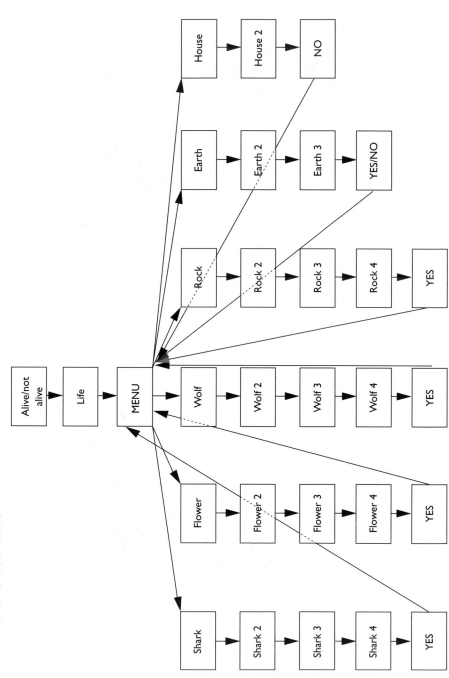

Figure A2.3 Plan for Alive and not alive.

4. Ancient Egypt

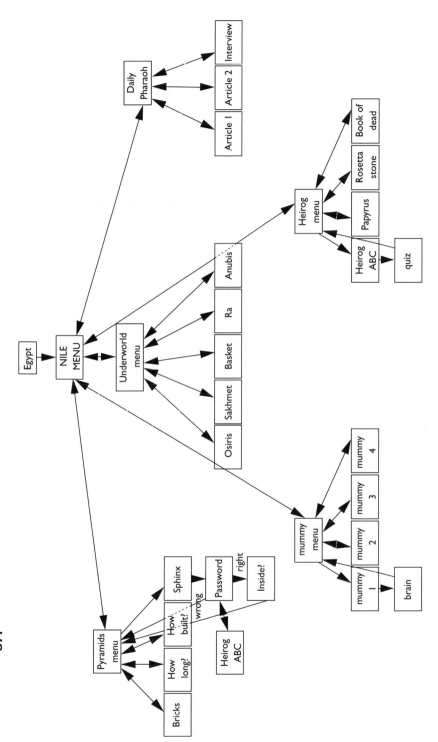

Figure A2.4 Plan for Ancient Egypt.

Appendix 3: Student-drawn plans

1. Alive and not alive: Year 3 (7–8 year olds)

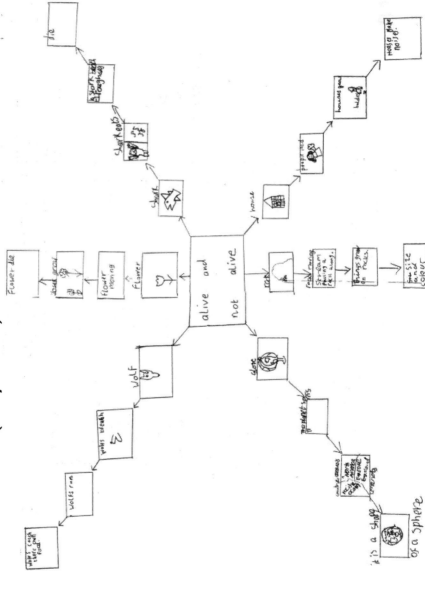

Figure A3.1 Student-drawn plan for Alive and not alive.

2. The Sun: Year 6 (10–11 year olds)

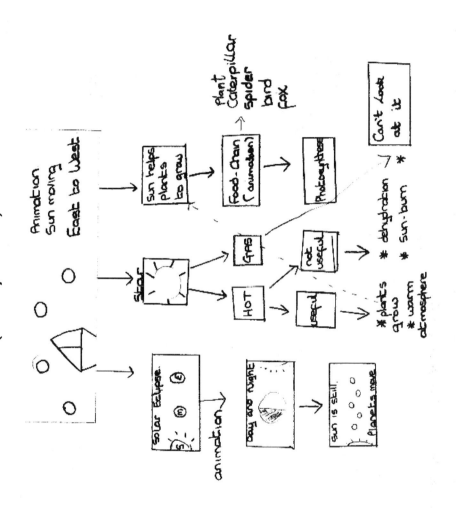

Figure A3.2 Student-drawn plan for The Sun.

Appendix 4: What is on the CD ROM

The CD ROM contains examples of multimedia work by Hackney students. There are some short sections taken from larger pieces of work and some whole multimedia projects. These can be used by students as an introduction to multimedia authoring, to analyse, to get ideas and to use as a basis for discussion and planning. The CD ROM can be accessed by specific subject, by chapter, or by title of multimedia presentation.

It will include information about Hackney, the author and where to get additional CD ROMs of Hackney students' work. There will be a link to an updated website for the book (**www.hackney-making-multimedia.org.uk**) where it will be possible to make comments and ask questions.

Chapter 1: Introduction

This will include the full presentation of:

> *The Tudor maze*   History, year 6 (10 and 11 year olds)

Chapter 2: Planning a project into the curriculum

This will include the four presentations from different curriculum areas:

> *Find the tigers*   English, year 6 (10 and 11 year olds)
> *Digestion and blood circulation*   Science, year 8 (12 and 13 year olds)
> *Persephone*   History, year 3 (7 and 8 year olds)
> *Find the climate*   Geography, year 5 (9 and 10 year olds)

Chapters 5, 7 and 8: Student presentations for critical analysis

These four pieces can be used in the classroom for analysis in terms of structure, audience and interactivity; their structures are in Appendix 2.

> *Alive and not alive*   Science, year 3 (7 and 8 year olds)
> *Ancient Egypt*   History, years 5/6 (9–11 year olds)
> *Alien from space*   Literacy, year 4 (8 and 9 year olds)
> *The water cycle*   Science, year 6 (10 and 11 year olds)

Chapter 5: Audience

This will include parts of presentations to demonstrate considerations of audience:

Wartime women   History, year 6 (10 and 11 year olds)
Evolution and inheritance   Science, year 10 (14 and 15 year olds)
Rainforests   Geography, year 6 (10 and 11 year olds)

Chapter 6: Designing screens

This will include individual screens from presentations to show elements of design, annotated text, integrated media and navigation.

Chapter 8: Interactivity

This chapter will show short examples of different sorts of on-screen interactivity.

Chapter 9: Collecting information and creating the presentation

This will show parts of several presentations to demonstrate the use of different media. It will also include the full presentations of two examples:

Greek myths and legends   History, year 5 (9 and 10 year olds)
Thorkel and Brynhild on board ship   History, year 4 (8 and 9 year olds)
The Periodic Table   Science, year 9 (13 and 14 year olds)
The Moon   Science, year 5 (9 and 10 year olds)

Chapter 13: Infants making multimedia

This will include the presentations described:

Here we are   Literacy, reception (4 and 5 year olds)
The computer children   Numeracy/literacy, year 1 (5 and 6 year olds)
Petsy   Literacy, year 2 (6 and 7 year olds)

Chapter 14: Special needs in primary schools

This will include the presentations described:

Animals in action   Science, years 5 and 6 (9–11 year olds)
Pollution   Science, year 4 (8 and 9 year olds)

Appendix 5: CD ROM running instructions

The minimum recommended machine specifications are:

PC	Mac
8Mb RAM (16Mb RAM recommended)	6Mb free RAM
Win 95 or higher	Mac OS 7.1 or higher

This CD ROM needs QuickTime™ installed on your computer to run.

To install QuickTime

QuickTime installers can be found on the CD in the following places:

- **PC** – Go to *My computer*: click on your CD drive: open the folder QuickTime Installer and double click on the icon QuickTime Installer.exe – follow on screen instructions.
- **Macintosh** – Open the QuickTime Installer folder: launch QuickTime Installer.

Alternatively you can visit the Apple Computer site on **http://www.apple.com** and download the latest versions of Quicktime.

Display settings on the PC should be set to High Colour. It will run on 256 colours but there may be problems with some images and animations.

To start the CD

- **PC** – Will start automatically. Remember to have QuickTime installed.
- **Macintosh** – Double click on CD icon
Double click on *Making Multimedia* icon

To quit the CD ROM

The CD ROM is linked up to return to the main menu from all title pages. If you need to quit mid-program at any time this can be done by:

- **PC** – Alt and F4
- **Macintosh** – Apple and Q

Appendix 6: Multimedia words

Button – or hotspot   A programmable area of the screen.

Card   A multimedia screen or page.

Hypermedia   Screens of multimedia linked together in a non-linear way.

Hypertext   Text which acts as a link when clicked on with a mouse.

ICT   Information and Communication Technology. This is a curriculum subject in the National Curriculum of England and Wales.

Interactive   The two-way communication between multimedia authors and their audience. This may be in the form of the user 'doing' something to use the piece, such as click, drag, type and make decisions.

Multimedia   Combination of three or more media from text, graphics, sound, animation and video. This can be linear or non-linear.

Non-linear   Non-sequential. A multimedia presentation that does not run as a linear narrative. This non-linearity is sometimes called associative.

Stack   A multimedia file of screens linked together.

References

Beichner, Robert J. (1994) 'Multimedia Editing to Promote Science Learning', *Journal of Computers in Mathematics and Science Teaching*, vol. 13, no. 2, pp. 147–62.

Harel, I. and Papert, S. (1990) 'Software Design as a Learning Environment', *Interactive Learning Environments*, vol. 1, pp. 1–32.

Hay, K., Gudzial, M., Jackson, S., Boyle, R. and Soloway, E. (1994) 'Students as Multimedia Composers', *Computers Education*, vol. 23, no. 4, pp. 301–17.

Heppell, Stephen (1994) 'Multimedia and Learning: Normal Children, Normal Lives and Real Change', in Underwood, Jean (ed.) *Computer Based Learning Potential into Practice*, pp. 156–62. London: David Fulton.

Kafai, Y., Ching, C. and Marshall, S. (1997) 'Children as Designers of Educational Multimedia Software', *Computers Education*, vol. 29, nos 2/3, pp. 117–26.

Lachs, Vivi (1995) 'Making the Computer Dance to your Tune: Authoring Hypermedia in Primary Schools', unpublished Masters thesis, King's College, London.

Lachs, Vivi (1999) 'The Moving Picture Science Show: Working with Multimedia in the Classroom', in Sefton-Green, Julian (ed.) *Young People, Creativity and New Technologies: The Challenge of Digital Arts*, pp. 12–21. London: Routledge.

Lachs, Vivi and Wiliam, Dylan (1998) 'Making the Computer Dance to Your Tune: Primary School Pupils Authoring Hypermedia', *Journal of Computing in Childhood Education*, vol. 9, no. 1, pp. 55–77.

Lafer, Stephen (1996) 'Audience, the Computer, and the Development of Writing Ability', *Computers in the Schools*, vol. 12, nos 1/2, pp. 141–52.

Lehrer, R., Erickson, J. and Connell, T. (1994) 'Learning by Designing Hypermedia Documents', *Computers in the Schools*, vol. 10, nos 1/2, pp. 227–54.

Liu, M. and Rutledge, K. (1997) 'The Effect of a "Learner as Multimedia Designer" Environment on At-Risk High School Students' Motivation and Learning of Design Knowledge', *Journal of Educational Computing Research*, vol. 16, no. 2, pp. 145–77.

McGill, I. and Weil, S. (1989) 'Continuing the Dialogue: New Possibilities for Experiential Learning', in Weil, S. and McGill, I. (eds) *Making Sense of Experiential Learning*. Buckingham: The Society for Research into Higher Education and The Open University Press.

McGrath, D., Cumaranatunge, C., Ji, M., Chen, H., Broce, W. and Wright, K. (1997) 'Multimedia Science Projects: Seven Case Studies', *Journal of Research on Computing in Education*, vol. 30, no. 1, pp. 18–37.

O'Neill, Bill (1998) 'New Ways of Telling: Multimedia Authoring in the Classroom', in Montieth, M. (ed.) *IT for Learning Enhancement*, pp. 141–52. Exeter: Intellect.

Palumbo, D. and Bermudez, A. (1994) 'Using Hypermedia to Assist Language Minority Learners in Achieving Academic Success', *Computers in the Schools*, vol. 10, nos 1/2, pp. 171–88.

Papert, S. (1991) 'Situating Constructionism', in Harel, I. and Papert, S. (eds) *Constructionism*, pp. 1–11. Boston, MA: MIT Media Laboratory.

Plowman, Lydia (1996) 'Narrative, Linearity and Interactivity: Making Sense of Interactive Multimedia', *British Journal of Educational Technology*, vol. 27, no. 2, pp. 92–105.

Reader, W. and Hammond, N. (1994) 'Computer Based Tools to Support Learning from Hypertext: Concept Mapping Tools and Beyond', *Computers Education*, vol. 22, nos 1/2, pp. 99–106.

Snyder, Ilana (1997) 'Hyperfiction: Its Possibilities in English', *English in Education*, vol. 31, no. 2, pp. 23–33.

Squires, D.J. (1996) 'Can Multimedia Support Constructivist Learning?', *Teaching Review*, vol. 4, no. 2, pp. 10–17.

Turner, S.V. and Handler, M.G. (1997) 'Hypermedia in Education: Children as Audience or Authors?' *Journal of Information Technology for Teacher Education*, vol. 6, no. 1, pp. 25–35.

Underwood, J. (1998) 'Making Groups Work', in Montieth, M. (ed.) *IT for Learning Enhancement*, pp. 29–41. Exeter: Intellect.

Vygotsky, L. (1978) *Mind in Society: The Development of Higher Psychological Processes.* Cambridge, MA: Harvard University Press.

Williams, Noel (1998) 'Educational Multimedia: Where's the Interaction?', in Montieth, M. (ed.) *IT for Learning Enhancement*. Exeter: Intellect.

Wisnudel, M. (1994) 'Constructing Hypermedia Artifacts in the Math and Science Classroom', *Journal of Computers in Mathematics and Science Teaching*, vol. 13, no. 1, pp. 5–15.

Wood, D.J., Bruner, J.S. and Ross, G. (1976) 'The Role of Tutoring in Problem Solving', *Journal of Child Psychology and Psychiatry*, vol. 17, pp. 89–100.

CD-ROM User Licence Agreement

We welcome you as a user of the *Making Multimedia in the Classroom: A Teacher's Guide* CD-ROM and hope that you find it a useful and valuable tool. Please read this document carefully. **This is a legal agreement** between you (hereinafter referred to as the "Licensee") and RoutledgeFalmer (the "Publisher") which defines the terms under which you may use the Product. By opening the package containing the CD-ROM you have agreed to these terms and conditions outlined herein. If you do not agree to these terms you must return the Product to RoutledgeFalmer intact with all its components as listed on the back of the package, within ten days of purchase and the purchase price will be refunded to you.

1. Definition of the Product

The product which is the subject of this Agreement, the *Making Multimedia in the Classroom: A Teacher's Guide* CD-ROM (the "Product") consists of:

1.1   Underlying data comprised in the product (the "Data")

1.2   A compilation of the Data (the "Database")

1.3   Software (the "Software") for accessing and using the Database

1.4   A CD-ROM disk (the "CD-ROM")

2. Commencement and Licence

2.1   This Agreement commences upon the breaking open of the package containing the CD-ROM by the Licensee (the "Commencement Date").

2.2   This is a licence agreement (the "Agreement") for the use of the Product by the Licensee, and not an agreement for sale.

2.3   The Publisher licenses the Licensee on a non-exclusive and non-transferable basis to use the Product on condition that the Licensee complies with this Agreement. The Licensee acknowledges that it is only permitted to use the Product in accordance with this Agreement.

3. Installation and Use

3.1 The Licensee may provide access to the Product only on a single personal computer for individual study. Mult-user use or networking is only permissible with the express permission of the Publisher in writing and requires paymen of the appropriate fee as specified by the Publisher, and signature by the Licensee of a separate multi-user licence agreement.

3.2 The Licensee shall be responsible for installing the Product and for the effectiveness of such installation.

3.3 Text from the Product may be incorporated in a coursepack. Such use is only permissible with the express permission of the Publisher in writing and requires the payment of the appropriate fee as specified by the Publisher and signature of a separate licence agreement.

4. Permitted Activities

4.1 The Licensee shall be entitled:

4.1.1 to use the Product for its own internal purposes;

4.1.2 to download onto electronic, magnetic, optical or similar storage medium reasonable portions of the Database provided that the purpose of the Licensee is to undertake internal research or study and provided that such storage is temporary;

4.1.3 to make a copy of the Database and/or the Software for back-up/archival/ disaster recovery purposes.

4.2 The Licensee acknowledges that its rights to use the Product are strictly as set out in this Agreement, and all other uses (whether expressly mentioned in Clause 5 below or not) are prohibited.

5. Prohibited Activities

The following are prohibited without the express permission of the Publisher:

5.1 The commercial exploitation of any part of the Product.

5.2 The rental, loan (free or for money or money's worth) or hire purchase of the product, save with the express consent of the Publisher.

5.3 Any activity which raises the reasonable prospect of impeding the Publisher's ability or opportunities to market the Product.

5.4 Any provision of services to third parties using the Product, whether by way of trade or otherwise.

5.5   Any networking, physical or electronic distribution or dissemination of the product save as expressly permitted by this Agreement.

5.6   Any reverse engineering, decompilation, disassembly or other alteration of the Software save in accordance with applicable national laws.

5.7   The right to create any derivative product or service from the Product save as expressly provided for in this Agreement.

5.8   The use of the Software separately from the Database.

5.9   Any alteration, amendment, modification or deletion from the Product, whether for the purposes of error correction or otherwise.

5.10   The merging of the Database or the Software with any other database or software.

5.11   Any testing, study or analysis of the Software save to study its underlying ideas and principles.

6. General Responsibilities of the Licensee

6.1   The Licensee will take all reasonable steps to ensure that the Product is used in accordance with the terms and conditions of this Agreement.

6.2   The Licensee acknowledges that damages may not be a sufficient remedy for the Publisher in the event of breach of this Agreement by the Licensee, and that an injunction may be appropriate.

6.3   The Licensee undertakes to keep the Product safe and to use its best endeavours to ensure that the product does not fall into the hands of third parties, whether as a result of theft or otherwise.

6.4   Where information of a confidential nature relating to the product or the business affairs of the Publisher comes into the possession of the Licensee pursuant to this Agreement (or otherwise), the Licensee agrees to use such information solely for the purposes of this Agreement, and under no circumstances to disclose any element of the information to any third party save strictly as permitted under this Agreement. For the avoidance of doubt, the Licensee's obligations under this sub-clause 6.4 shall survive termination of this Agreement.

7. Warrant and Liability

7.1   The Publisher warrants that it has the authority to enter into this Agreement, and that it has secured all rights and permissions necessary to enable the Licensee to use the Product in accordance with this Agreement.

7.2   The Publisher warrants that the CD-ROM as supplied on the Commencement Date shall be free of defects in materials and workmanship, and undertakes to replace any defective CD-ROM within 28 days of notice of such defect being received provided such notice is received within 30 days of such supply. As an alternative to replacement, the Publisher agrees fully to refund the Licensee in such circumstances, if the Licensee so requests, provided that the Licensee returns the Product to the Publisher. The provisions of this sub-clause 7.2 do not apply where the defect results from an accident or from misuse of the product by the Licensee.

7.3   Sub-clause 7.2 sets out the sole and exclusive remedy of the Licensee in relation to defects in the CD-ROM.

7.4   The Publisher and the Licensee acknowledge that the Publisher supplies the Product on as "as is" basis. The Publisher gives no warranties:

7.4.1   that the Product satisfies the individual requirements of the Licensee; or

7.4.2   that the product is otherwise fit for the Licensee's purpose; or

7.4.3   that the Data is accurate or complete or free of errors or omissions; or

7.4.4   that the product is compatible with the Licensee's hardware equipment and software operating environment.

7.5   The Publisher hereby disclaims all warranties and conditions, express or implied, which are not stated above.

7.6   Nothing in this Clause 7 limits the Publisher's liability to the Licensee in the event of death or personal injury resulting from the Publisher's negligence.

7.7   The Publisher hereby excludes liability for loss of revenue, reputation, business, profits, or for indirect or consequential losses, irrespective of whether the Publisher was advised by the Licensee of the potential of such losses.

7.8   The Licensee acknowledges the merit of independently verifying Data prior to taking any decisions of material significance (commercial or otherwise) based on such data. It is agreed that the Publisher shall not be liable for any losses which result from the Licensee placing reliance on the Data or on the database, under any circumstances.

7.9   Subject to sub-clause 7.6 above, the Publisher's liability under this Agreement shall be limited to the purchase price.

8. Intellectual Property Rights

8.1   Nothing in this Agreement affects the ownership of copyright or other intellectual property rights in the Data, the Database, the Software or the Manual.

8.2   The Licensee hereby agrees to abide by copyright and similar notice requirements required by the Publisher, details of which are as follows: "©2000 RoutledgeFalmer, an imprint of the Taylor & Francis Group, and its licensors. All Rights Reserved. All materials in the *Making Multimedia in the Classroom: A Teacher's Guide* CD-ROM are copyright protected. No such materials may be used, displayed, modified, adapted, distributed, transmitted, transferred, published or otherwise reproduced in any form or by any means now or hereafter developed other than strictly in accordance with the terms of the licence agreement enclosed with the CD-ROM. However, text may be printed and copied for research and private study within the preset program limitations. Please note the copyright notice above, and that any text or images printed or copied must credit the source."

8.3   This Product contains material proprietary to and copyrighted by the Publisher and others. Except for the licence granted herein, all rights, title and interest in the Product, in all languages, formats and media throughout the world, including all copyrights therein, are and remain the property of the Publisher or other copyright owners identified in the Product.

9. Non-assignment

This Agreement and the licence contained within it may not be assigned to any other person or entity without the written consent of the Publisher.

10. Termination and Consequences of Termination

10.1   The Publisher shall have the right to terminate this Agreement if:

10.1.1 the Licensee is in material breach of this Agreement and fails to remedy such breach (where capable of remedy) within 14 days of a written notice from the Publisher requiring it to do so; or

10.1.2 the Licensee becomes insolvent, becomes subject to receivership, liquidation or similar external administration; or

10.1.3 the Licensee ceases to operate in business.

10.2   The Licensee shall have the right to terminate this Agreement for any reason upon two months' written notice. The Licensee shall not be entitled to any refund for payments made under this Agreement prior to termination under this sub-clause 10.2.

10.3   Termination by either of the parties is without prejudice to any other rights or remedies under the general law to which they may be entitled, or which survive such termination (including rights of the Publisher under sub-clause 6.4 above).

10.4   Upon termination of this Agreement, or expiry of its terms, the Licensee must:

10.4.1 destroy all back up copies of the product; and

10.4.2 return the Product to the Publisher.

11. General

11.1 *Compliance with export provisions*
The Publisher hereby agrees to comply fully with all relevant export laws and regulations of the United Kingdom to ensure that the Product is not exported, directly or indirectly, in violation of English law.

11.2 *Force majeure*
The parties accept no responsibility for breaches of this Agreement occurring as a result of circumstances beyond their control.

11.3 *No waiver*
Any failure or delay by either party to exercise or enforce any right conferred by this Agreement shall not be deemed to be a waiver of such right.

11.4 *Entire agreement*
This Agreement represents the entire agreement between the Publisher and the Licensee concerning the Product. The terms of this Agreement supersede all prior purchase orders, written terms and conditions, written or verbal representations, advertising or statements relating in any way to the Product.

11.5 *Severability*
If any provision of this Agreement is found to be invalid or unenforceable by a court of law of competent jurisdiction, such a finding shall not affect the other provisions of this Agreement and all provisions of this Agreement unaffected by such a finding shall remain in full force and effect.

11.6 *Variations*
This Agreement may only be varied in writing by means of variation signed in writing by both parties.

11.7 *Notices*
All notices to be delivered to: RoutledgeFalmer, 11 New Fetter Lane, London EC4P 4EE, UK.

11.8 *Governing law*
This Agreement is governed by English law and the parties hereby agree that any dispute arising under this Agreement shall be subject to the jurisdiction of the English courts.

If you have any queries about the terms of this licence, please contact:

RoutledgeFalmer
11 New Fetter Lane
London EC4P 4EE
Tel: *44 (0)20 7583 9855
Fax: *44 (0)20 7842298
Email: <info@tandf.co.uk>

The CD-ROM

The accompanying *Making Multimedia in the Classroom: A Teachers' Guide* CD-ROM contains examples of student work described in the book.

Instructions for running the CD-ROM can be found in Appendix 5 above.

For terms of use of the CD-ROM, please see the CD-ROM User Licence Agreement on pp. 194–9 above.

CD-ROM Copyright © 2000 RoutledgeFalmer and its licensors

HyperStudio® Copyright © 1993–2000 Roger Wagner Publishing, Inc. All Rights Reserved

The multimedia environment of this software is provided by HyperStudio®, a product of Roger Wagner Publishing, Inc.

Made with QuickTime™

QuickTime and the QuickTime logo are trademarks under licence.

HyperStudio® is a registered trademark of Knowledge Adventure, Inc.

HyperStudio Player (a run-time version of the copyrighted computer program HyperStudio®), Licensed to Taylor & Francis Books Ltd to distribute only in combination with *Making Multimedia in the Classroom: A Teachers' Guide* by Vivi Lachs. HyperStudio Player may not be copied onto another diskette, except for archive purposes, or into memory unless part of the execution of *Making Multimedia in the Classroom: A Teachers' Guide*. When *Making Multimedia in the Classroom: A Teachers Guide* has completed execution, HyperStudio Player shall not be used to execute any other program.

ROGER WAGNER PUBLISHING, INC. MAKES NO WARRANTIES, EITHER EXPRESS OR IMPLIED, REGARDING THE ENCOLOSED COMPUTER SOFTWARE PACKAGE, ITS MERCHANTABILITY OR ITS FITNESS FOR ANY PARTICULAR PURPOSE. THE EXCLUSION OF IMPLIED WARRANTIES IS NOT PERMITTED IN SOME STATES. THE ABOVE EXCLUSION MAY NOT APPLY TO YOU. THIS WARRANTY PROVIDES YOU WITH SPECIFIC LEGAL RIGHTS. THERE MAY BE OTHER RIGHTS THAT YOU MAY HAVE WHICH VARY FROM STATE TO STATE.